PHANTOM 3 STANDARD

BASIC REFERENCE

(based on DJI Manual V1.4 & DJI GO App, Android Version 2.8.1)

DJI Phantom 3 Standard

BASIC REFERENCE

(based on DJI Manual V1.4 & DJI GO App, Android Version 2.8.1)

ISBN-10: 1530798795
ISBN-13: 978-1530798797

First Printing, June 2016

KAHALA PRESS
P.O. Box 26451
Honolulu, HI 96825

PREFACE

This booklet is written for beginning pilots who are interested in flying the DJI Phantom 3, Standard Model. This booklet is meant to supplement the DJI manual, not replace it. The DJI manual and this booklet share much of the same information, but there are still significant differences between them not only in terms of content but in how that content is organized and presented. In short, you can benefit by studying both.

The information contained in here is current as of June 2016 and is for educational purposes only. The DJI Manual, V1.4, and DJI GO app, Android Version 2.8.1, served as the primary references.

This booklet can also be used for the iOS version of the GO app, v2.8.3, but there are a few minor differences, which are noted on pages 114-117.

This booklet offers several recommendations, but this does not mean there is only one way of doing or understanding things. For instance, this booklet has a preflight checklist, but as you gain knowledge and experience, you might very well create your own checklist. Ultimately, you must use your judgement and experience in deciding the best way to do things.

Great care was taken to ensure the accuracy of the information in this book; however, if you happen to notice any errors or have any suggestions for improvement, please contact us at admin@dji.server808.net.

Best of luck and please fly safely.

Greg Keast
June 2016

CONTENTS

INTRODUCTION

The DJI GO App is a sophisticated program that lies at the heart of flying the Phantom 3 Standard. A solid working knowledge of it is essential to operating the aircraft and getting the most out of it.

This section covers the basic steps of getting started with the program.

The first step is to download the app to your mobile device. The DJI Manual comes with a QR code that makes it easy to download the app. You will need to have a barcode scanner app on your phone in order to do this.

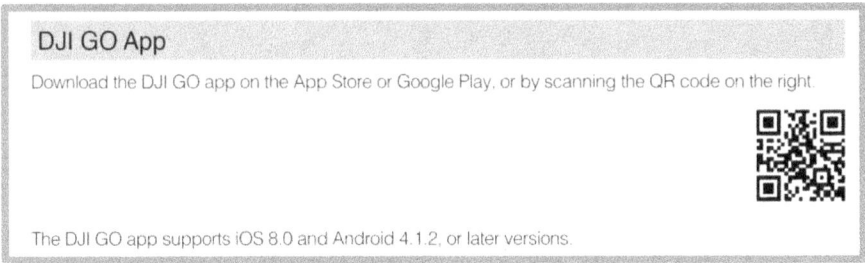

DJI GO App

Download the DJI GO app on the App Store or Google Play, or by scanning the QR code on the right.

The DJI GO app supports iOS 8.0 and Android 4.1.2, or later versions.

Once the app is installed, tap the DJI icon to launch it.

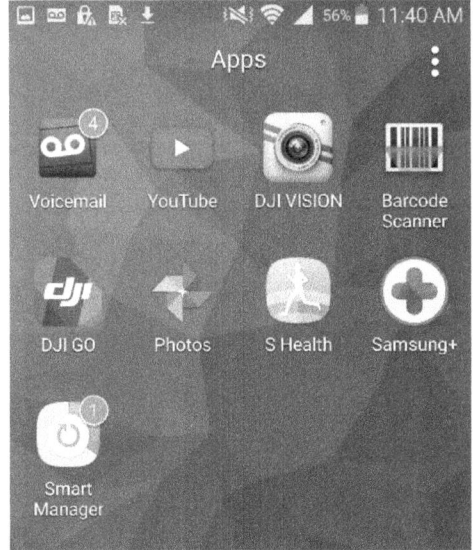

Since the app is used for other DJI products, the Phantom 3 Standard is not the first aircraft that might appear. Swipe through the pages to find the Phantom 3 series, then arrow down to get to the Standard.

If the "Enter Camera View" button is gray, then that means the aircraft is not connected to your mobile device.

To connect to the Phantom's Wi-Fi signal, you need to go to the Wi-Fi Settings on your mobile device and look for the Phantom connection. The password to connect should be on the bottom of the remote controller.

Once connected, the "Enter Camera View" button should be blue and confirms the Wi-Fi connection.

From the Intro Screen, you can also access Flight Records and the DJI Flight Simulator, which is a part of the DJI Academy.

FLIGHT RECORD

Favorite	Date	Location	Mileage	Time	Max Alt	Photos	Video	Footage
	05:49:58	Map Loading	6052.8ft	22Min	135.2ft	0	00:00	
	09/05/2016	Map Loading	5272.1ft	14Min	119.1ft	2	00:00	
	08/05/2016	Map Loading	339.7ft	7Min	42.0ft	0	03:23	
	08/05/2016	Map Loading	102.6ft	4Min	12.8ft	0	00:00	
	08/05/2016	Map Loading	163.5ft	3Min	67.9ft	1	00:00	
	08/05/2016	Map Loading	64.1ft	3Min	4.3ft	1	00:00	
	06/05/2016	Map Loading	6130.2ft	13Min	319.9ft	1	00:00	

The Flight Record keeps a running log of information about the flights you have made.

ACADEMY / FLIGHT SIMULATOR

The Academy has a flight simulator and access to manuals and video tutorials. The flight simulator requires you to power on the remote and aircraft. For safety, DJI recommends removing the propellers before using the simulator.

 # BATTERY SETTINGS

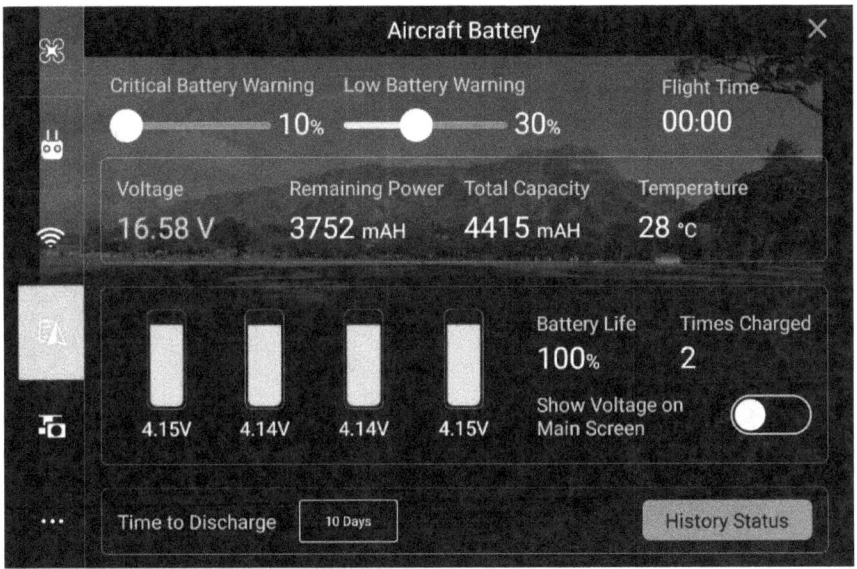

Battery settings are accessed through the Battery Settings icon on the Main Screen or through the General Settings in the upper-right corner of the Main Screen. (see Front Cover)

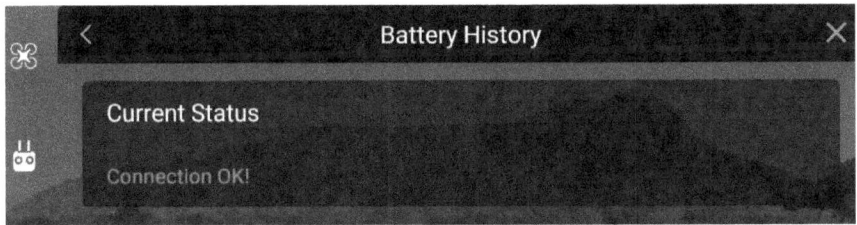

There are four settings you can adjust on the battery.

1. Critical Battery Warning (10% to 50%).
2. Low Battery Warning (15% to 50%).
3. Display Voltage on Main Screen.
4. Time to Discharge (1 to 10 days).

 # BATTERY SETTINGS

IF LED IS FLASHING,
THE MINIMUM REMAINING POWER IS:

0%   25%   50%   75%

The exact Battery Level is also prominently displayed on the Main Screen. (see Front Cover)

NOTES:

If the battery level is above 95%, turn on the battery before charging; otherwise, it will not fully charge. (page 18, DJI Manual)

Discharge the battery down to less than 8% (or to when it can't be turned on) at least once every 20 charges. Do not discharge to zero. The percentage of charge can be checked on the Aircraft Battery screen on the DJI GO app.

The battery discharges to below 65% if left idle for more than 10 days. Press the Power Button once to restart the 10-day timer.

Do not recharge until the battery has cooled down.

COMPASS CALIBRATION

The compass requires calibration to ensure optimal flight performance. However, it is important to do the calibration in a wide-open area far from anything man-made or natural that might cause electromagnetic interference. This also includes small things you might carry such as car keys or a cell phone. DJI recommends compass calibration at *every new flight location;* however, some pilots say this is not necessary and warn that an improperly done calibration is worse than updating an older, properly done one. A system status alert may also notify you when a calibration is needed.

1. Tap on the System Status Bar to bring up the Status window.

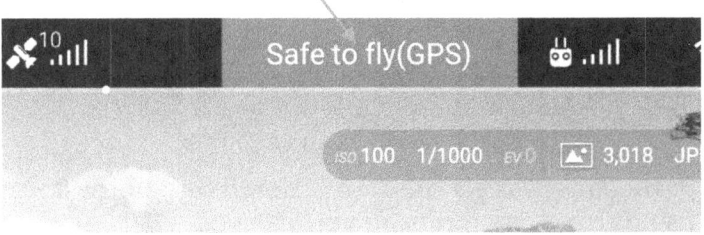

2. Tap on the Calibrate button and then tap OK.

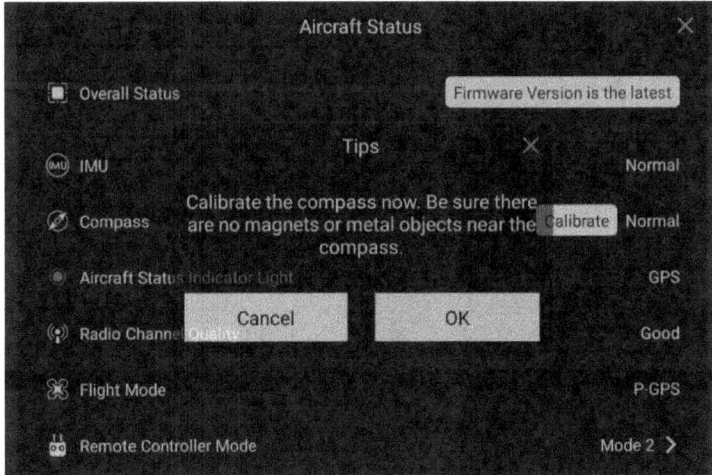

3. Follow the on-screen directions. Note: You can spin the craft around in your hands. The aircraft must stay in the same spot but rotates around the imaginary axis line.

4. Be sure the aircraft is pointed nose down and holds its position as it is rotated along the vertical axis.

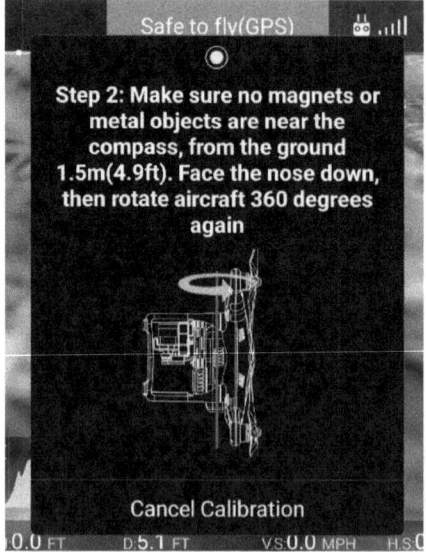

FIRMWARE UPDATES

For the DJI Phantom 3 Standard, all firmware updates are done through the GO app. The app will remind you when an update is due and will also walk you through the process with a series of message screens.

You initiate the Update simply by tapping on Update Now.

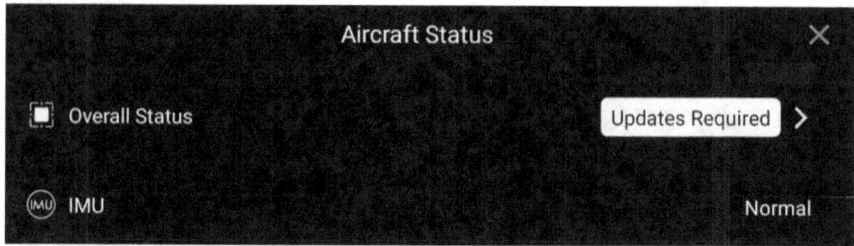

Overall Status   Updates Required   ›

IMU   Normal

You will also receive a notification about updates through the System Status screen.

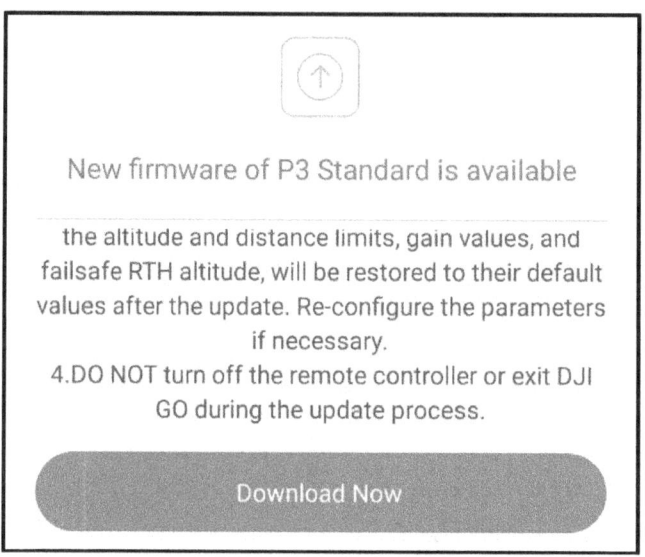

New firmware of P3 Standard is available

the altitude and distance limits, gain values, and failsafe RTH altitude, will be restored to their default values after the update. Re-configure the parameters if necessary.
4.DO NOT turn off the remote controller or exit DJI GO during the update process.

Download Now

After you initiate the Update process, you should see a screen similar to the one above. It will tell you what changes the update will make, then advise you not to turn off the remote controller during the process.

It should be noted that before you do an update, you need to make sure the aircraft, remote, and mobile device are all fully charged.

On average, the update process can take anywhere from 15-30 minutes.

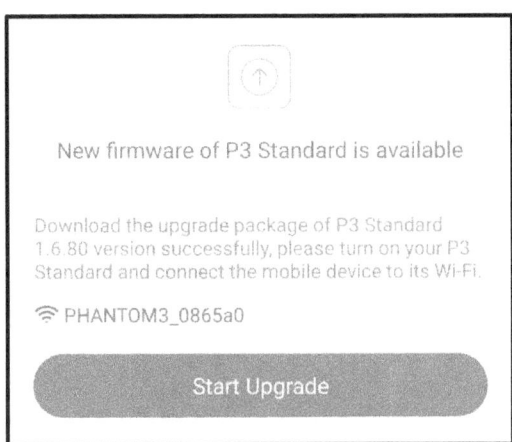

New firmware of P3 Standard is available

Download the upgrade package of P3 Standard
1.6.80 version successfully, please turn on your P3
Standard and connect the mobile device to its Wi-Fi.

📶 PHANTOM3_0865a0

Start Upgrade

Once you have finished downloading the update, you might need to configure your Wi-Fi settings back to the aircraft itself. After everything is on and connected, then you can tap on the Start Upgrade button.

During the update, the status lights on the aircraft's camera will flash red and green, and you will hear a series of beeps.

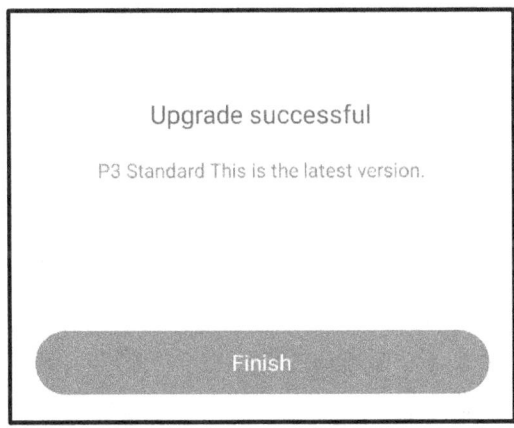

Upgrade successful

P3 Standard This is the latest version.

Finish

Once the update is done, the message above should appear on your mobile device, and you are done.

It is important to stay current with all the latest updates. Some of them fix critical errors. If you are flying with old firmware, you are taking an unnecessary risk.

FLASHING LIGHTS

AIRCRAFT LED STATUS LIGHTS

AIRCRAFT LED STATUS LIGHTS
(located in back of craft)

The two red lights on the front of the aircraft are for visual navigation and can be turned off. The lights in the back indicate the status of the aircraft.

When the lights are slowly flashing green or yellow, then that means the aircraft is safe to fly. Flashing red means the battery is running low, and steady red is a critical error. Please refer to the back cover of the book for a reference chart.

AIRCRAFT STATUS INDICATOR IN DJI GO APP

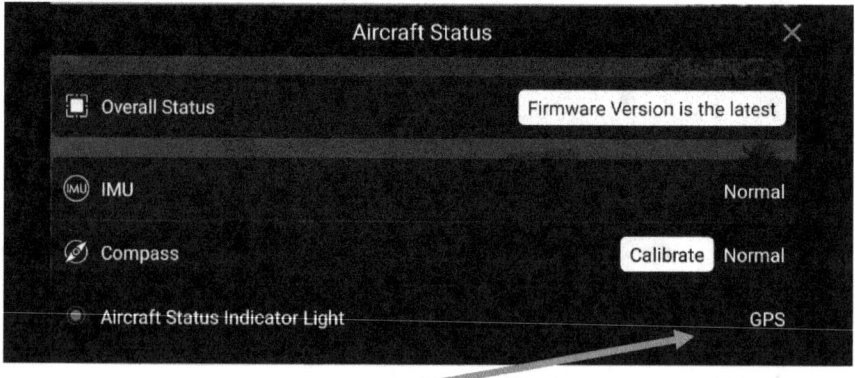

Displays the type of message. In this case, it is advising that the status light relates to the GPS signal.

GPS SIGNAL & FLIGHT WARNINGS

MESSAGE	FLASHING LIGHT
STRONG GPS SIGNAL	GREEN
WEAK GPS SIGNAL	YELLOW
NO FLY OR RESTRICTED ZONE	RED

The Aircraft Status Indicator Light, as shown on page 16, can display the status of the craft from within the GO app.

REMOTE CONTROLLER STATUS LED

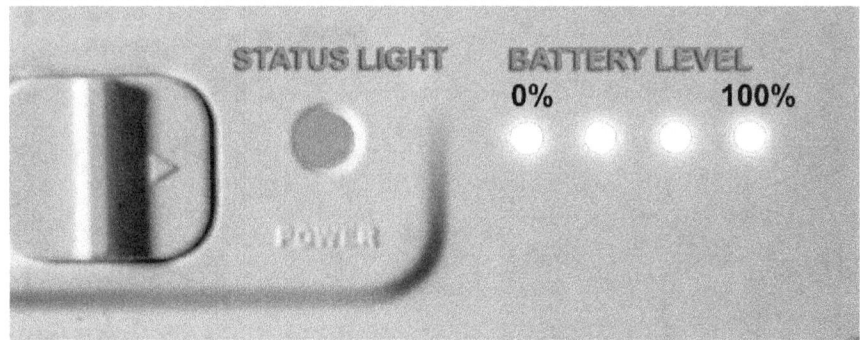

The Remote Control has a series of four lights that display the battery level. When the Remote Control starts running low on power, the Status Light will turn red. It will also begin making a beeping sound.

You always want to make sure you keep the remote control fully charged when you begin flying. If the battery dies on the remote and you lose contact with the aircraft, then the aircraft will initiate the Return-to-Home procedure, but you will have no way of controlling the aircraft manually and will be at the mercy of the Return-to-Home procedure.

CAMERA STATUS LED

CAMERA STATUS LED

The Camera Status LED is a very small light right above the camera. It is virtually impossible to see when the aircraft is flying, but it can be seen when the aircraft is very close.

MESSAGE	SIGNAL
WARMING UP	FAST GREEN FLASHES
SINGLE SHOT	SINGLE GREEN FLASH
BURST MODE	THREE GREEN FLASHES
RECORDING	SLOW RED FLASHES
SD CARD ERROR	FAST RED FLASHES
OVERHEATING	TWO RED FLASHES
SYSTEM ERROR	STEADY RED
FIRMWARE UPDATE	GREEN & RED FLASHES

BATTERY PROTECTION WARNINGS

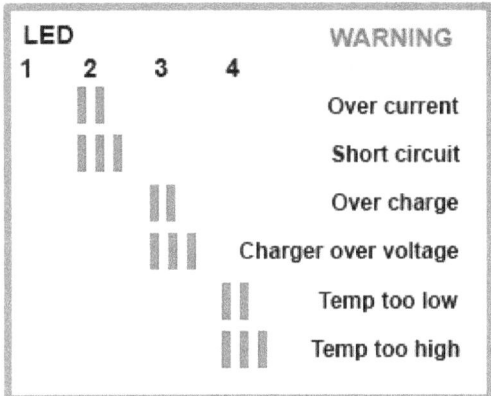

LED				WARNING
1	2	3	4	
	‖			Over current
	‖‖			Short circuit
		‖		Over charge
		‖‖		Charger over voltage
			‖	Temp too low
			‖‖	Temp too high

In addition to the Battery Protection Warnings that appear on the battery itself, you might also receive Battery Warnings through the GO app while in flight.

APP ALERT	ACTION NEEDED
OVER CURRENT	DO NOT FLY AGGRESSIVELY
OVER TEMPERATURE	AIRCRAFT WILL REDUCE POWER
HIGH/LOW TEMPERATURES	LAND IMMEDIATELY
CELL DAMAGE	STOP USING THE BATTERY

If you press the power button on the battery, and it only shows a solid red light and no green lights, then the battery is over discharged and is probably dead.

The battery's operating temperature is between 14 and 104 degrees Fahrenheit or between -10 and 40 degrees Celsius. Extreme temperatures reduce the performance and life of the battery and should be avoided. If the temperature exceeds 140 degrees Fahrenheit or 60 degrees Celsius, you should land immediately, and in cold weather, if you get a low battery alert, you should land as soon as possible.

FLIGHT MODES

There are three basic modes, which are set by the S1 switch on the remote control.

S1 SWITCH

P-MODE	**UP**
A-MODE	**CENTER**
F-MODE	**DOWN**

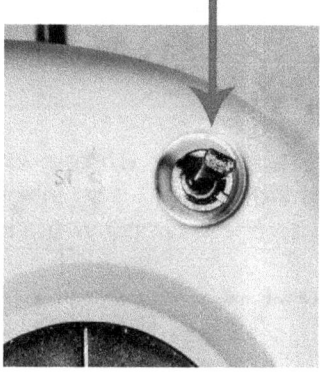

P-MODE (P-GPS)

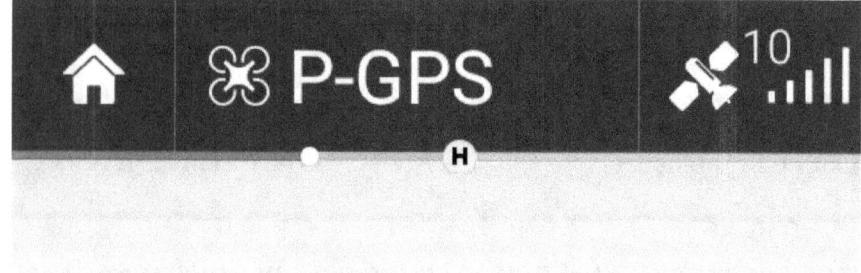

P-MODE has two operating conditions: *P-GPS, which uses GPS and P-ATTI, which does not.* The condition selected is automatically determined by the aircraft and depends on the strength of the GPS signal. If the signal is sufficient, then the aircraft will fly in P-GPS mode and will use GPS for positioning.

Note: A-MODE and F-MODE have to be enabled under Enable Multiple Flight Modes under Advanced settings.

P-MODE (P-ATTI)

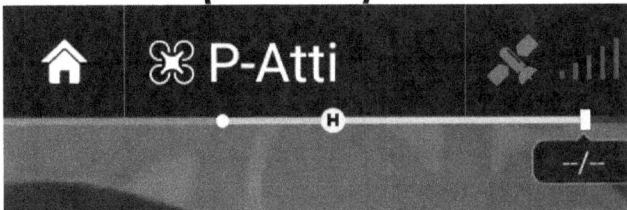

If the GPS signal is not present or sufficient, then the aircraft will fly in P-ATTI mode and does not use GPS for positioning. It only uses the aircraft's barometer.

A-MODE (ATTI)

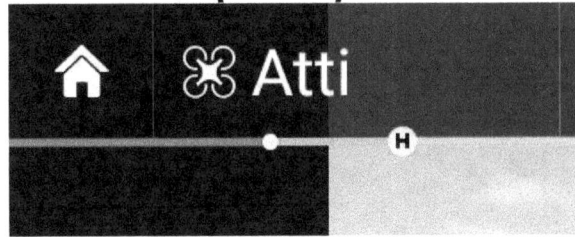

If set to A-MODE, the aircraft only uses its barometer to maintain altitude. In this mode, the aircraft will go in whatever direction the wind is blowing and does not use GPS positioning. Return-to-Home might still work if some GPS signal is available.

F-MODE (F-GPS)

If set to F-MODE, the Intelligent Flight or Navigation Modes are available. These are: Course Lock, Home Lock, Point of Interest, Follow Me, and Waypoints. The aircraft requires GPS to operate in this mode.

GENERAL CAMERA SETTINGS
PHOTOGRAPHY

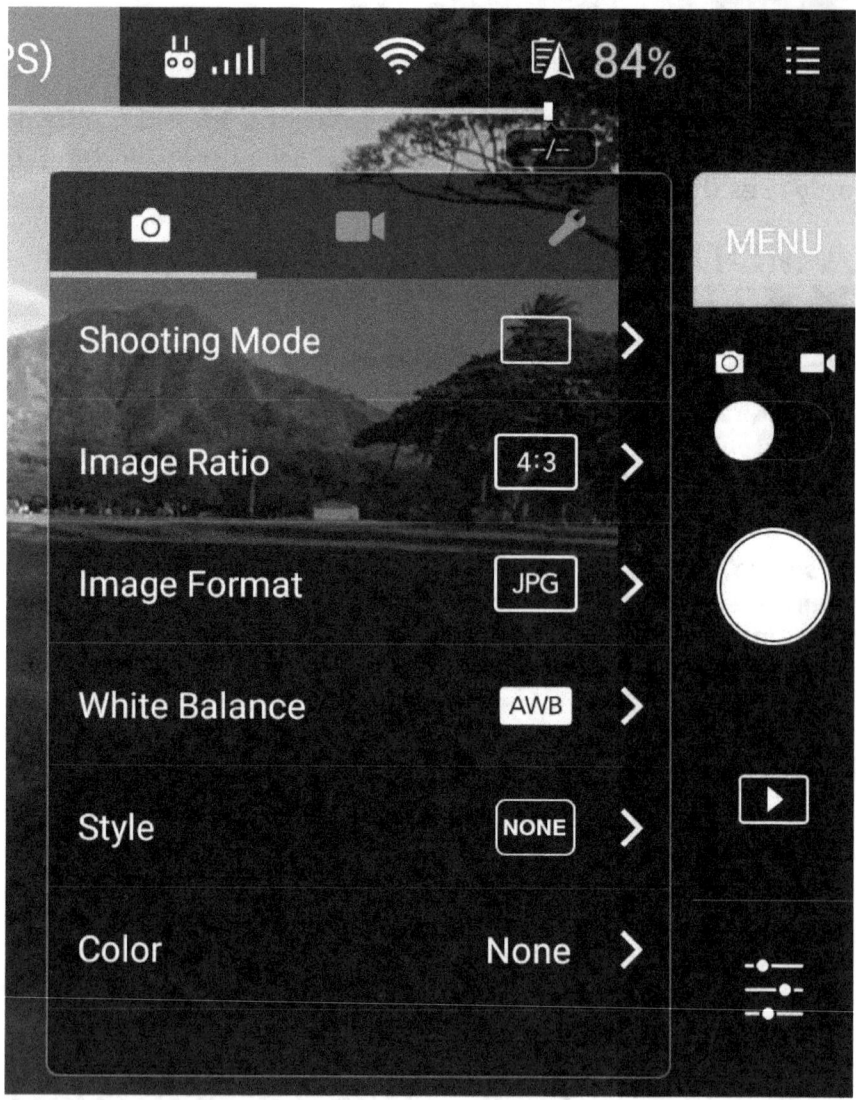

PHOTOGRAPHY
MENU OPTIONS AT A GLANCE

FIRST LEVEL	SECOND LEVEL	THIRD LEVEL
SHOOTING MODE >		
	SINGLE SHOT	
	HDR	
	BURST MODE >	
		3 / 5 / 7
	AEB >	
		3 / 5
	TIME LAPSE >	
		5 / 7 / 10 / 20 / 30
IMAGE RATIO >		
	4:3 / 16: 9	
IMAGE FORMAT >		
	JPG / RAW / JPG + RAW	
WHITE BALANCE >		
	AUTO	
	SUNNY	
	CLOUDY	
	INCANDESCENT	
	NEON	
	CUSTOM >	
		2,000 – 10,000 K
STYLE >		
	STANDARD	
	LANDSCAPE	
	SOFT	
	CUSTOM	
COLOR >		
	D-LOG	
	D-CINELIKE	
	NONE	
	ART	
	BLACK WHITE	
	VIVID	
	BEACH	
	DREAM	
	CLASSIC	
	NOSTALGIA	

SHOOTING MODE

Shooting Mode has five settings, which include single shot; high dynamic range (HDR); burst mode; automatic exposure bracketing (AEB); and time lapse. Of these five, burst mode, AEB, and time lapse give you additional setting options.

BURST MODE

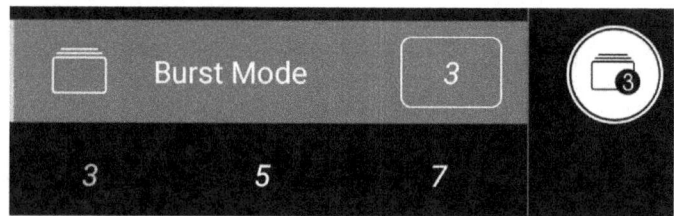

Burst mode takes a series of 3, 5, or 7 shots in rapid succession. Burst mode is typically used anytime a key or fast-moving action is occurring and the photographer wants to be sure he or she gets the best possible shot.

AUTOMATIC EXPOSURE BRACKETING

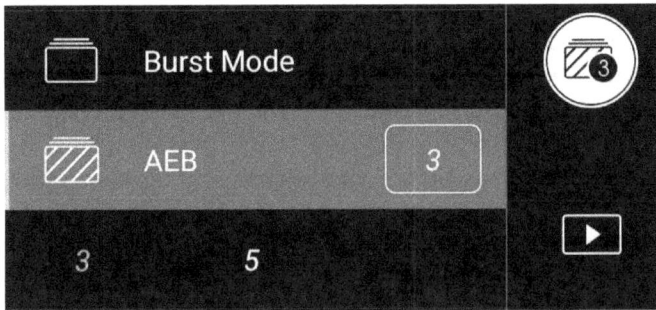

Automatic exposure bracketing takes the same shot 3 or 5 times at different exposure settings to make sure the shot is properly exposed. AEB is useful in situations where the lighting is susceptible to change or the photographer wants to have a range of exposures to choose from.

TIME LAPSE

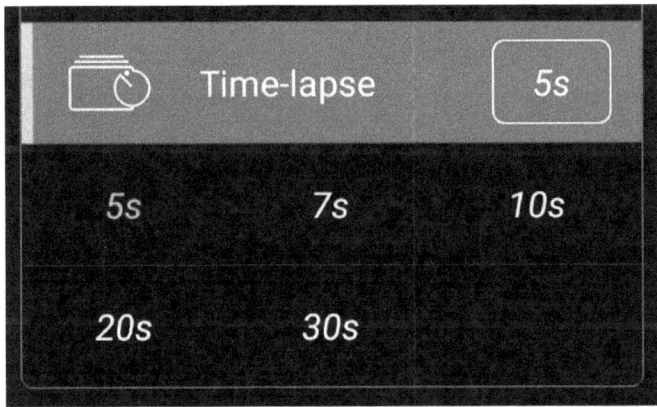

Please note that with a max flight time of approximately 25 minutes, the longest time-lapse video possible is about 10 seconds. If you are shooting at a 5-second interval, you would be getting 12 shots per minute, and 12 shots per minute x 25 minutes equals 300 total shots. If you play the rendered sequence at 30 frames per second, then 300 shots divided by 30 frames per second equals 10 seconds of time lapse.

TIME LAPSE GUIDELINES

In general, the faster the subject is moving, the faster the interval should be. If you are shooting traffic or crowds, then 5 seconds would probably be best. Clouds and sunsets could be within the 5-10 second range. Construction or slow-moving subjects should have a longer interval. Also, motion blur is usually desirable, so you want to consider shooting with a slower shutter speed, for example, below 1/100th of a second.

Please note that the slower your shutter speed, the greater the need for stabilization. It takes testing to find the exact settings that work for you.

IMAGE RATIO

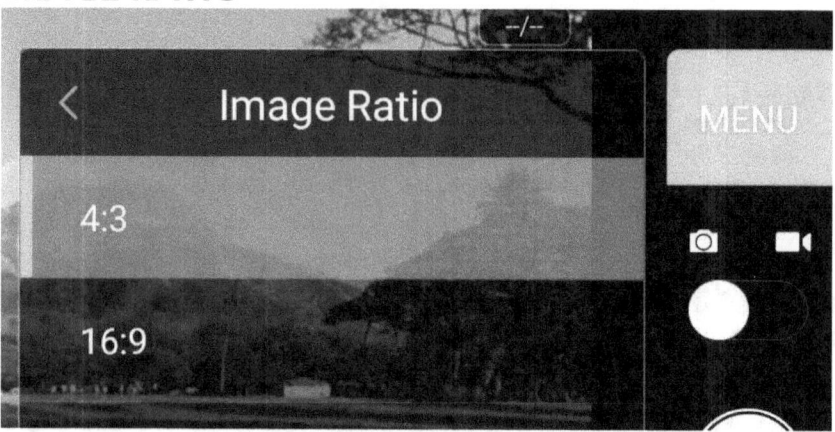

Image ratio sets the display aspect ratio for your image. Four by three (4:3) is not cropped and reflects the size of the sensor (4072 x 3046 pixels). Sixteen by nine (16:9) is cropped and is the aspect ratio most associated with high-definition televisions and computer monitors.

IMAGE FORMAT

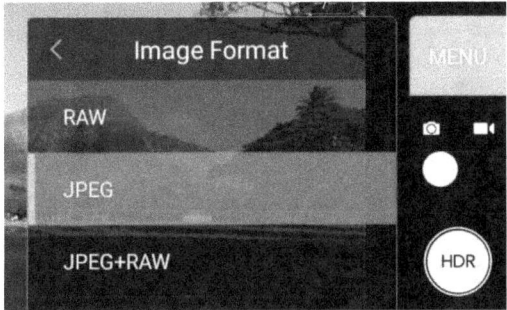

Image Format allows three ways to save your photo files: RAW (uncompressed), JPEG (compressed), or both. If you shoot in RAW, the image is saved as a .DNG file or digital negative. For high-quality photography, the preference is to shoot in RAW and color correct and grade the photos later in editing. If you want the convenience of being able to upload or email photos right away, then shooting in JPEG is a convenient option.

WHITE BALANCE

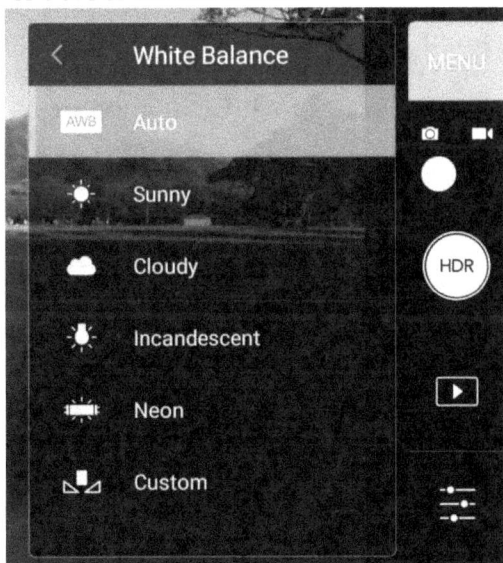

It is advisable to use one of the manual settings rather than AUTO. The AUTO setting will change as the color temperature does and can lead to inconsistency across images, especially when shooting video.

CUSTOM WHITE BALANCE

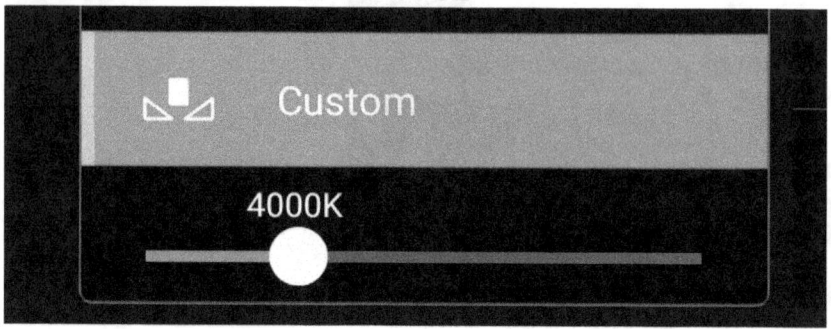

The Custom setting ranges from 2,000 to 10,000 K in increments of 100.

The table below provides general guidelines and are only approximate. Lower temperatures are warmer while higher temperatures are cooler.

It is also a good practice to take a picture or shoot video of a white balance card, so you have can have a precise point of reference if and when you are trying to color correct the image later. It takes a little time to do this, but it will pay off when you are editing and want to achieve a precise white balance.

COLOR TEMPERATURE (approximate)	
DEGREES (K)	CONDITIONS
1,900	Candlelight
2,500	Sunrise / Sunset
3,200	Incandescent/tungsten
4,000	Fluorescent
5,500	Standard daylight
6,500	Cloudy
7,000	Light shade
9,000	Deep shade
10,000	Blue sky

STYLE SETTINGS

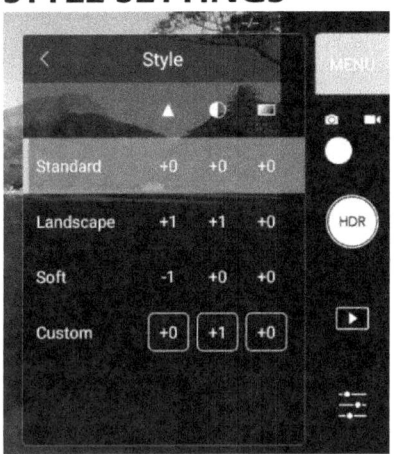

The Style Settings allow you to adjust sharpness, contrast, and saturation in your imagery. It comes with three preset settings: Standard, Landscape and Soft. Standard is neutral; Landscape increases both sharpness and contrast; and Soft only decreases sharpness. Style Settings apply to JPEG photos and to video but not to RAW photos or .DNG files.

STYLE SETTING	SHARPNESS	CONTRAST	SATURATION
Standard	0	0	0
Landscape	+1	+1	0
Soft	-1	0	0
Custom	User Defined Settings		

For the Custom Setting, you can set the style setting yourself. Many professional users decrease sharpness, contrast, and saturation by 2 or 3 points across the board.

COMMON CUSTOM SETTINGS

SHARPNESS	CONTRAST	SATURATION
-2	-1	-2
-2	-2	-2
-2	-3	-2

By decreasing these settings, you preserve more image data and increase the latitude you have when color correcting and grading; however, there are limits on how far you can push any image in terms of color correction and grading before it begins to break down. It is advisable to shoot test footage using different settings and decide for yourself which settings give you the image you want.

STANDARD
The Standard Style makes no adjustments to sharpness, contrast, or saturation. It is the equivalent of a Neutral Style.

LANDSCAPE
The Landscape Style gives a modest boost to sharpness and contrast and leaves saturation in a neutral position. These settings are thought to accentuate outdoor imagery, and they might as long as there is no extreme detail in the shot.

SOFT
The Soft Style applies a modest decrease in sharpness and helps to reduce aliasing (see below); however, a -1 decrease alone might not be sufficient.

CUSTOM
The Custom Setting allows you to choose your settings within the range of -3 to +3. It is highly recommended that you experiment with these settings to determine which settings give you the image quality you are looking for. It is best to start by adjusting one setting at a time, so you can see the effect of each setting individually.

ALIASING
Aliasing occurs when a camera's sensor sees repetitive detail (e.g., closely spaced lines, roof shingles, tight patterns, etc.) and cannot correctly process all the image data it receives and creates distortions that are not part of the actual image. Moiré and stair-stepping are examples of aliasing. Options to reduce or eliminate aliasing include not filming any imagery prone to aliasing, moving the camera closer (which adds space and reduces detail), or decreasing the sharpness (which creates blur and softens the aliasing effect).

COLOR SETTINGS

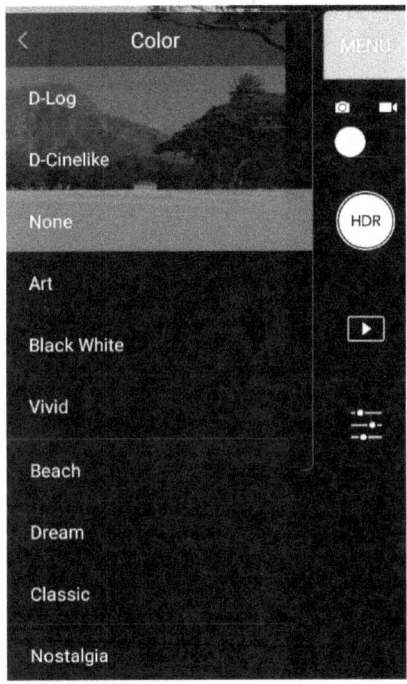

Most professionals shoot video in D-Log as this provides the greatest latitude when color correcting and grading. D-Log produces a flat and washed-out image, but it can be brought back to life with proper grading. The Color Settings are essentially for convenience because they provide ready-made grading styles that require minimal, if any, correction and grading. Shooting in D-Log is like baking a cake from scratch and gives you maximum creative control. Using the other settings is like using a cake mix from the store — most of the work is already done, but you can still tweak it if you want.

If you are knowledgeable about color correction and grading, then you can make D-Log footage look like any of the other styles with some adjustments. For instance, the ART setting is extremely desaturated while VIVID is overly saturated. The settings of NONE and D-CINELIKE give the least-stylized look and can be considered *realistic* in appearance. The truth is there is no right or wrong when it comes to style. These are settings for creative control and convenience.

QUICK SUMMARY OF COLOR SETTINGS

D-LOG
A flat, washed-out image, requires color grading.

D-CINELIKE
Applies a cinema-type gamma curve; this results in an image with more detail and less contrast; it is considered *film-like* in appearance; it does not necessarily require grading.

NONE
Applies no gamma or grading adjustments. Image can be used as is.

ART
Extremely desaturated image.

BLACK AND WHITE
Completely desaturated.

VIVID
Extremely saturated and *overcooked.*

BEACH
Color graded to emphasize sand and sky tones.

DREAM
A softer BEACH look.

CLASSIC
Moderate color grading and contrast.

NOSTALGIA
Sepia toning for an old-film look.

GENERAL CAMERA SETTINGS
VIDEO

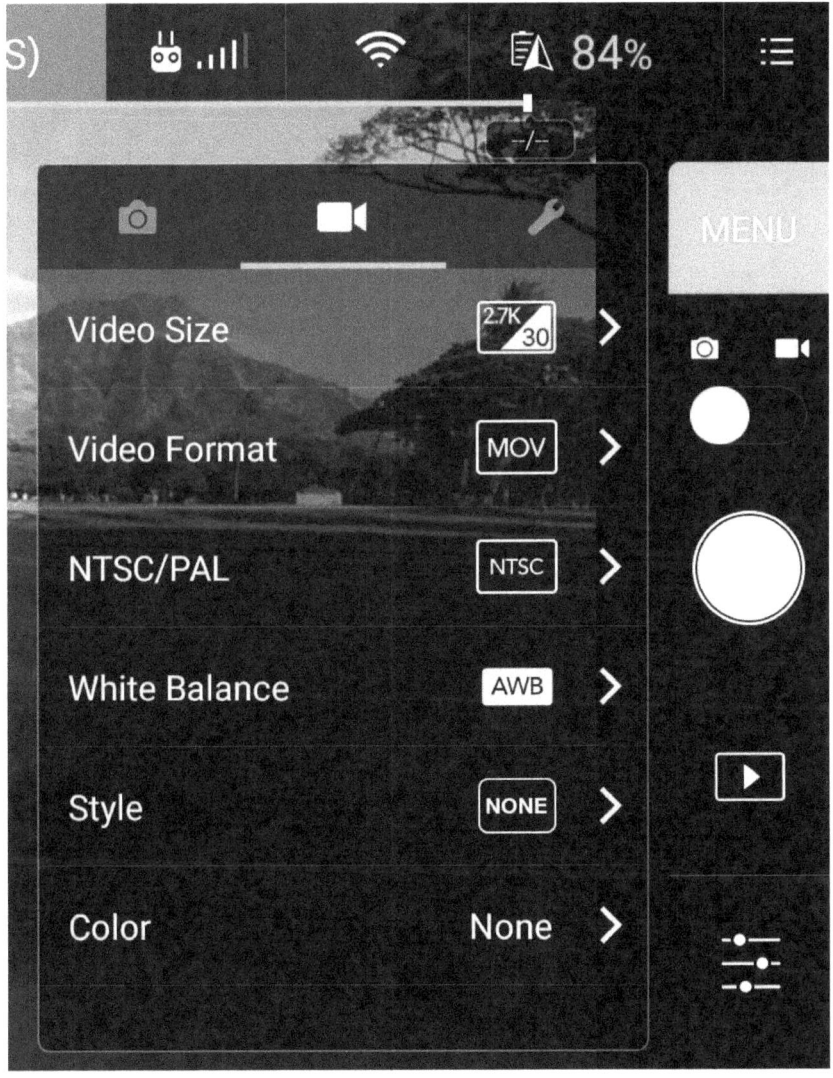

VIDEO
MENU OPTIONS AT A GLANCE

FIRST LEVEL	SECOND LEVEL	THIRD LEVEL
VIDEO SIZE >		
	2.7 K >	
		24 / 30 fps
	1080P >	
		24 / 30 fps
	720P >	
		24 / 30 / 48 / 60 fps
VIDEO FORMAT >		
	MOV / MP4	
NTSC / PAL >		
	NTSC / PAL	
WHITE BALANCE >		
	AUTO	
	SUNNY	
	CLOUDY	
	INCANDESCENT	
	NEON	
	CUSTOM >	
		2,000 – 10,000 K
STYLE >		
	STANDARD	
	LANDSCAPE	
	SOFT	
	CUSTOM	
COLOR >		
	D-LOG	
	D-CINELIKE	
	NONE	
	ART	
	BLACK WHITE	
	VIVID	
	BEACH	
	DREAM	
	CLASSIC	
	NOSTALGIA	

VIDEO SIZE (2.7K)

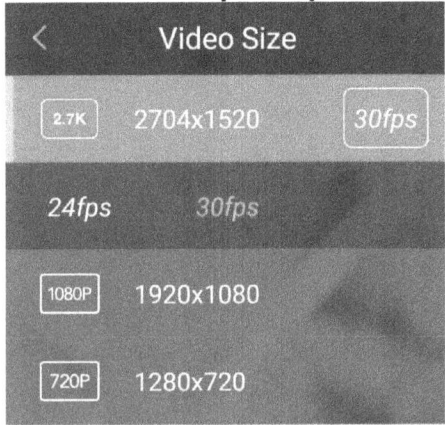

The camera can record video at 2.7K, but for most productions, this footage will have to be converted down to 1920 by 1080, which is High Definition. Shooting at 2.7K and down-converting provides a higher-quality image and more flexibility in editing than shooting in 1080p alone.

VIDEO SIZE (1080p)

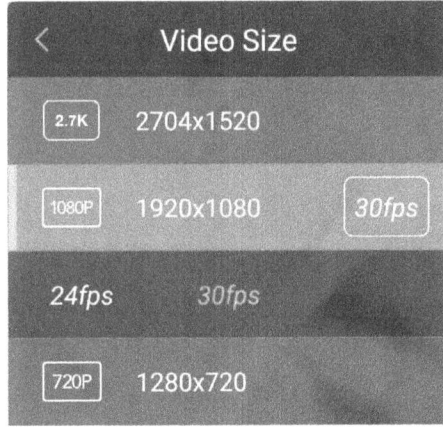

For 1080p, you only have the option to shoot at either 24 or 30 fps. Twenty-four frames-per-second (fps) is typically associated with the film look while 30 fps is associated with a more commercial or video look. If you want to shoot 1080p at 60 frames per second, you will have to upgrade to the Phantom 3 Advanced, the next model above the Standard.

VIDEO SIZE (720p)

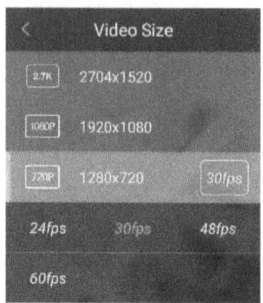

With 720p, you are given the highest frame rate this model of camera shoots at, which is 60 fps. Higher frame rates are helpful if you want to slow the footage later in postproduction. All the video sizes are considered wide-screen, but are susceptible to letter boxing if they are edited as a 4:3 project or displayed on a standard-definition television.

LETTER BOXING

This can occur when wide-screen video (16:9) is played on a standard or full-screen (4:3) display. It can also occur when 16:9 footage is imported into a video-editing program and rendered out as a standard-definition or 4:3 project.

PILLAR BOXING

This can occur when standard-definition video (4:3) is played on a wide-screen (16:9) TV. It can also occur when 4:3 footage is imported into a video-editing program and rendered out as a wide-screen or 16:9 project.

(photo credit: Leo Benini CC 3.0)

VIDEO FORMAT

This setting gives you a choice of the video container and is simply a preference with regard to your editing software. Some software works better with .mov files while others work better with .mp4 files. There is no significant difference in video quality or file size with either video format. Each container houses the same video codec.

BROADCAST STANDARDS

This setting should be chosen based on where you are planning to broadcast your video. If you are shooting for North America and parts of South America, then you would choose NTSC; if you are shooting for Europe and many other places in the world, then you would choose PAL.

It is always a good idea to consider the market for which you will be distributing your footage.

If you are considering selling or using your footage in Europe and North America, then it would be advisable to shoot two versions of everything (one in PAL and one in NTSC) on separate SD cards. Always begin with the end in mind.

GENERAL CAMERA SETTINGS
TOOLS

TOOLS
MENU OPTIONS AT A GLANCE
FIRST LEVEL   SECOND LEVEL

SHOW HISTOGRAM

VIDEO CAPTION

OVEREXPOSURE

SHOW GRID >

                    OFF
                    GRID LINES
                    GRID + DIAGONALS
                    CENTER POINT

ANTI-FLICKER >

                    50 Hz / 60 Hz

FILE INDEX MODE >

                    RESET / CONTINUOUS

RESET CAMERA SETTINGS

FORMAT SD CARD

SHOW HISTOGRAM

OVEREXPOSED, POOR DYNAMIC RANGE

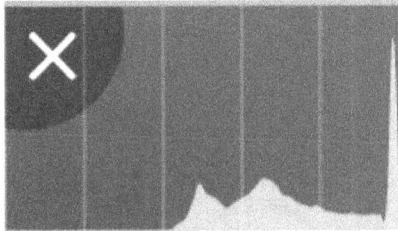

PROPER EXPOSURE, GOOD DYNAMIC RANGE

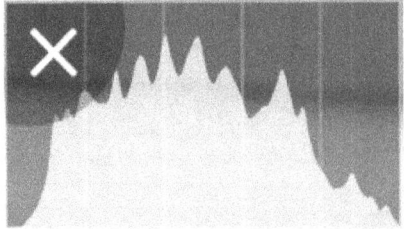

UNDEREXPOSED, POOR DYNAMIC RANGE

The histogram shows the distribution of tonal values from total black (0) on the left to total white (255) on the right. A properly exposed image spans the entire length of the graph. If there is a lack of data on the left, then the image is overexposed and lacks darker values. If there is a lack of data on the right, then the image is underexposed and lacks brighter values. It is usually best to expose to the right, which means you want the right endpoint to come as close to the right edge as possible without touching it. If the image data goes beyond either the left or right edge, then that data is not usually recoverable. When shooting in RAW or D-LOG mode, the histogram might not accurately reflect the true dynamic range you have actually captured, so it may be of less help.

VIDEO CAPTION

DJI_0006	5/8/2016 5:05 PM	MP4 Video	496,197 KB
DJI_0006.SRT	5/8/2016 5:05 PM	SRT File	33 KB
DJI_0007	5/8/2016 5:12 PM	MP4 Video	842,020 KB
DJI_0007.SRT	5/8/2016 5:12 PM	SRT File	55 KB

When you turn Video Caption on, a separate .SRT file is created along with the video file. This file contains flight and camera data, which displays as a subtitle when the video is played on certain video players. To get the caption or subtitle to display, you must pair the .SRT file with the video file. For instance, if you are using the VLC Media Player, which is available for free as a download, you would follow these steps:

1. Go to Open Media, then to Open File.

2. Click Add, then browse to the video file you wish to play. After you add the video file, then you can check the "Use a subtitle file" box and select the associated .SRT file.

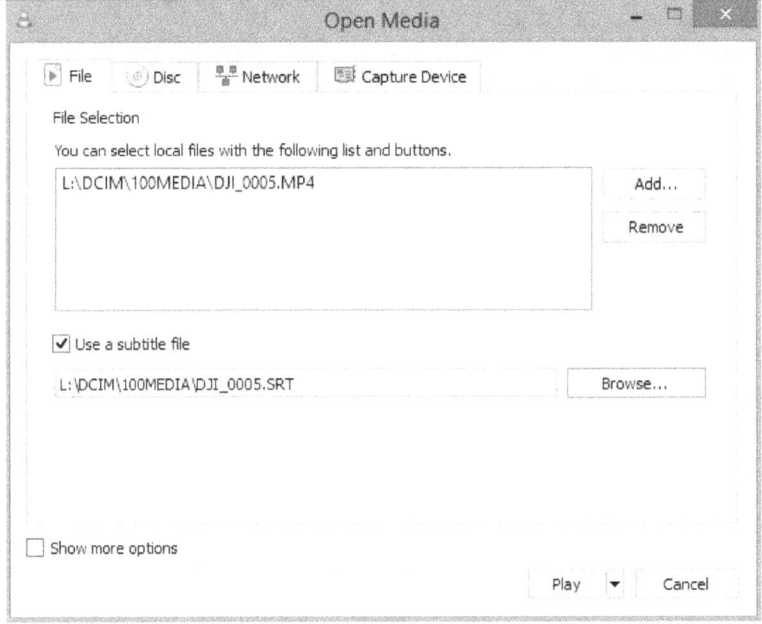

3. Once you play the video, then the flight and camera data will display as a subtitle or caption on the video.

OVER EXPOSURE WARNING

This setting displays zebra lines whenever an overexposure occurs. If you have the camera set to Auto Exposure, a yellow circle also appears. If you touch on any part of the image, the circle will move to that spot and exposure will be adjusted for that area of the image. However, it is not recommended that you use Auto Exposure when shooting video as it changes the shutter speed and ISO settings and can adversely affect image quality.

NEUTRAL DENSITY FILTERS

Unless you are planning to shoot video exclusively at dusk, dawn, or in low light, then you will need to get Neutral Density (ND) filters for the camera. You do not need filters for photos, only video.

A sunny day will usually require a 4 or 5-stop ND filter, and even a cloudy day can require a 2 or 3-stop filter.

DJI does not make ND filters for the Phantom 3 Standard; however, DitzCo of Chicago, Illinois sells an ND filter kit for $28.95. It uses circular filters that can be snapped to the front of the lens with a precisely fitted ring. For readers of this book, enter the promo code 15OFFBOOK to receive a 15% discount. Visit DITZCO.COM for more information about the kit.

Note: Only install ND filters with the aircraft off.

SHOW GRID

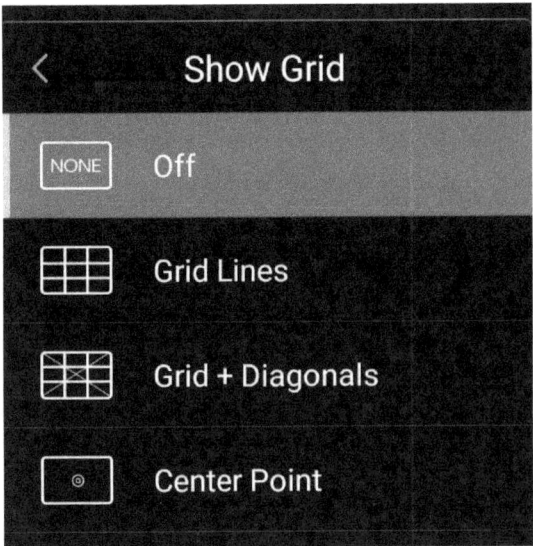

Show Grid allows you to superimpose lines or markers that assist with composition and tracking. The general theory is that shots are more visually appealing when the primary subject is off center or where the lines of the grid intersect. With that said, there are times when it is completely appropriate to frame the primary subject in the center as well.

GRID LINES

GRID LINES AND DIAGONALS

CENTER POINT

ANTI-FLICKER

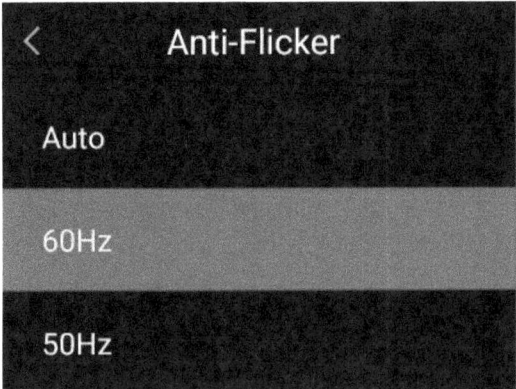

Anti-Flicker reduces flickering upon video playback. It should match the NTSC or PAL settings you have chosen. If you are shooting in the United States, then it should be set to NTSC, and Anti-Flicker should be set to 60Hz. If you are shooting in Europe, then it should be set to PAL, and Anti-Flicker should be set to 50Hz.

FILE INDEX MODE

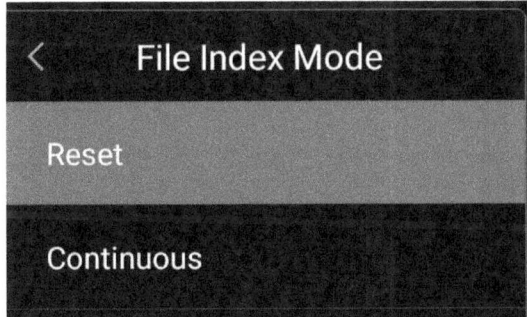

When File Index Mode is set to *Reset*, the photo and video file numbering system *resets* each time the aircraft is turned off. When it is set to *Continuous*, the files are continuously numbered in a sequence no matter how many times the aircraft is powered off and on.

GIMBAL

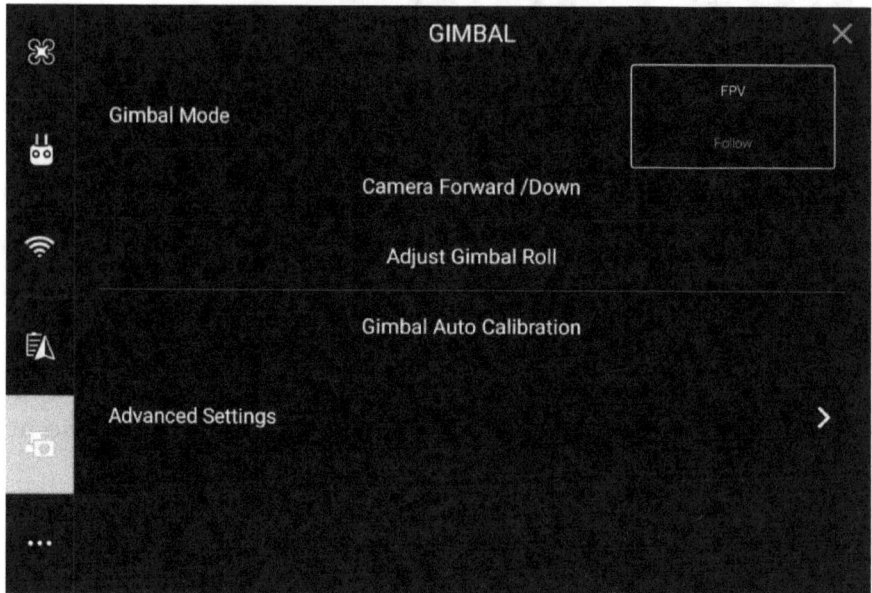

GIMBAL MODE
Two settings choices: First Person View (FPV), which essentially locks the gimbal in place and allows someone to see the aircraft as if from the position of flying it.

Follow Mode allows the gimbal to remain consistently level no matter the position of the aircraft.

CAMERA FORWARD / DOWN
This button lets you switch between the camera facing straight forward or straight down. The change happens instantly.

GIMBAL ROLL ADJUST

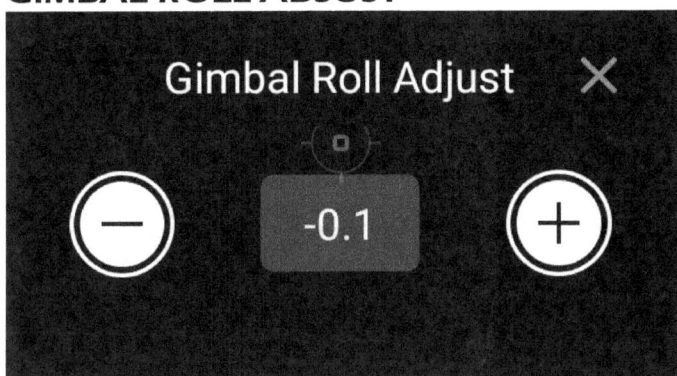

This setting lets you manually adjust the gimbal's tilt from side to side. This can be useful if you are shooting video, and the horizon is not level in the shot. Normally, if the gimbal is calibrated correctly, it will stay level, but if the aircraft is fighting against the wind, this type of adjustment might be helpful.

GIMBAL AUTO CALIBRATION

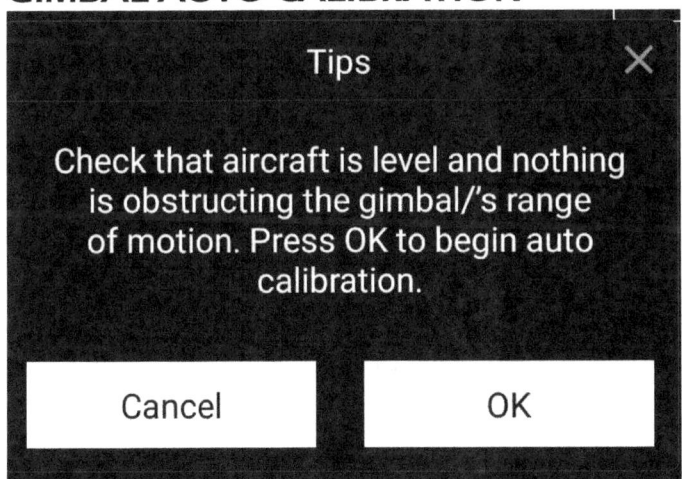

Auto Calibration resets the gimbal to a level horizon, but the aircraft itself must be on a level surface to calibrate properly.

ADVANCED SETTINGS

These settings help provide a fine level of control over gimbal movement. The gimbal moves in two basic directions. It can tilt up or down (pitch) or it can pan from right to left or left to right (yaw). Based on your shooting needs and preferences, you can store three configurations with different settings.

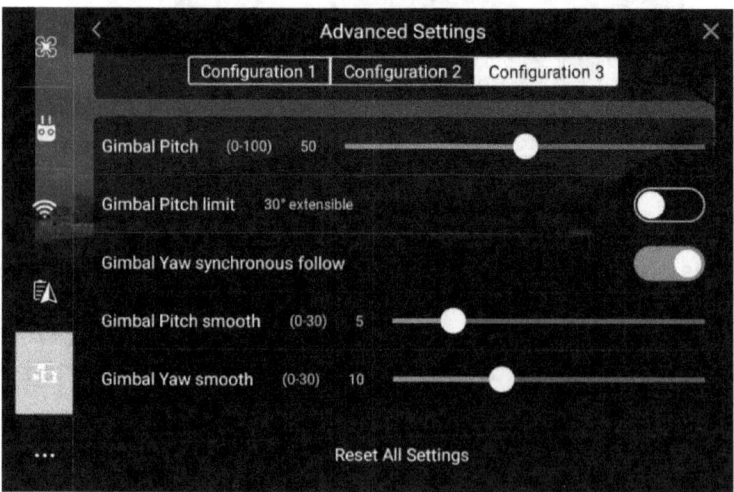

GIMBAL PITCH

This controls the responsiveness of the gimbal's tilt. It adjusts in single increments from 0 to 100. The higher the number, the faster the gimbal responds.

GIMBAL PITCH LIMIT

Allows the gimbal to tilt up another 30 degrees.

GIMBAL YAW SYNCHRONOUS FOLLOW

When this setting is on, the control stick for yaw also turns the gimbal slightly in the same direction. This allows the camera to gently pan with the rotation of the aircraft. This has the effect of cushioning the camera's movement and creating smoother panning shots. When this setting is off, the stick only controls yaw and the gimbal tightly tracks with the rotation of the aircraft. The effect of this setting is rather subtle, so sometimes it can be hard to tell if it is turned on without checking it.

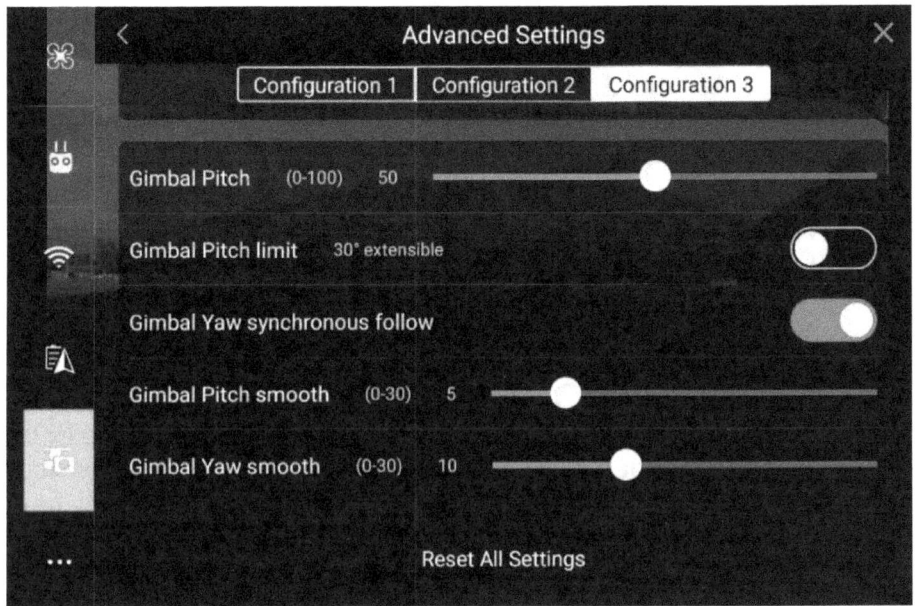

GIMBAL PITCH SMOOTH
Controls the abruptness at which the gimbal stops when tilting up or down. It adjusts in single increments from 0 to 30. The higher the number, the more of a rolling stop the gimbal has. At a lower setting, the gimbal stops immediately.

GIMBAL YAW SMOOTH
Controls the abruptness at which the gimbal comes to a stop when panning. It adjusts in single increments from 0 to 30. The higher the number, the more rolling stop the gimbal has. At a lower setting, the gimbal stops immediately.

Note: When adjusting these settings, you can experiment with them without flying. You will need to power on the aircraft, but do not need to start the motors. Just be sure the gimbal lock is off and it is safe to do so.

HOME POINTS

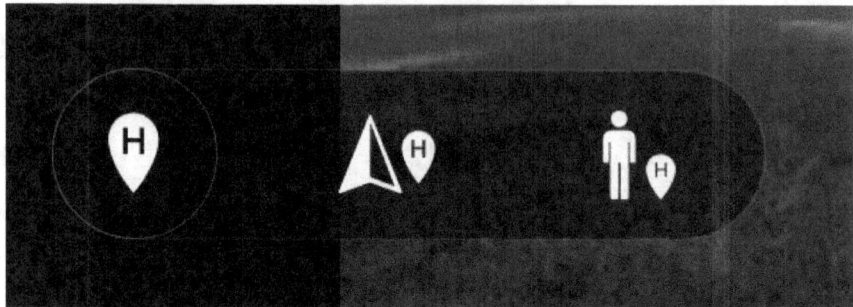

SETTING THE HOME POINT

As a part of your preflight routine, make sure your Home Point is updated at each new location. It is important to remember that during a Failsafe Return-to-Home, the aircraft will land within 65 feet of the Home Point and might not land exactly where you planned; therefore, you need to make certain that when you set a Home Point, there is plenty of space for the aircraft to land in an emergency.

If you do not select a Home Point, the operating system will occasionally update it automatically. You may also hear an automated message confirming the update. Setting the Home Point every time you fly is something you should do as part of your standard preflight procedures.

HOME POINT SET TO AIRCRAFT

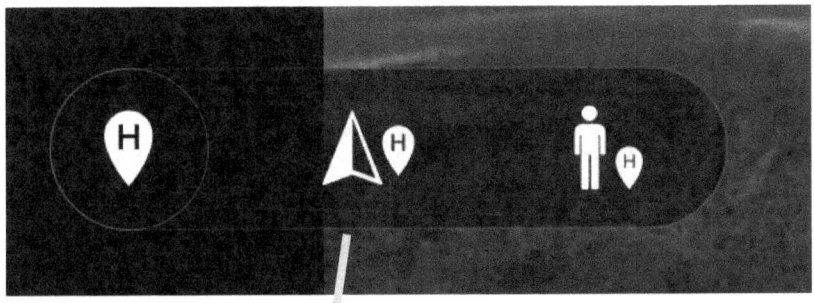

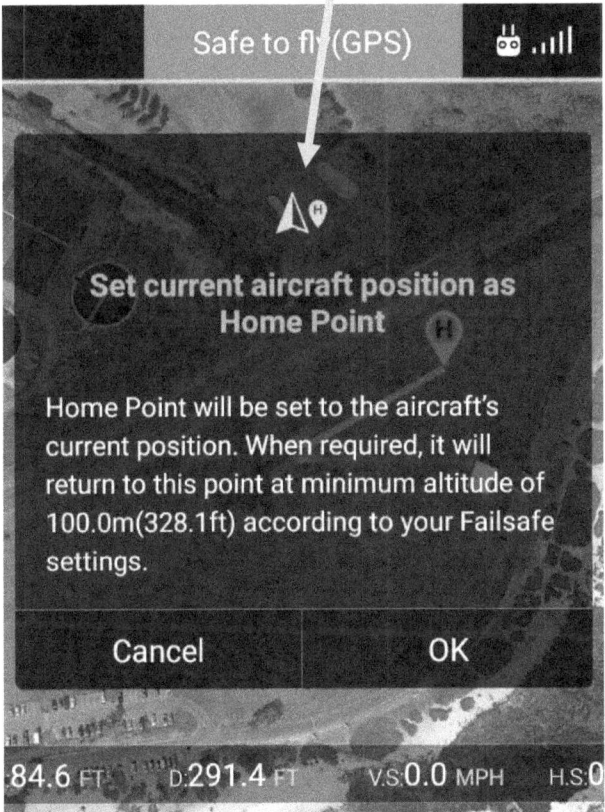

When you select the Aircraft Icon, the above screen will display, and you can set the Home Point to the Aircraft's current position or cancel it.

HOME POINT SET TO MOBILE DEVICE

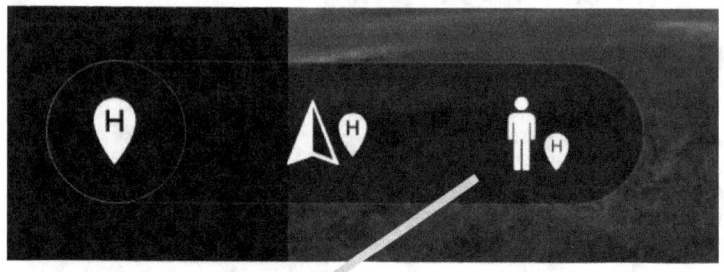

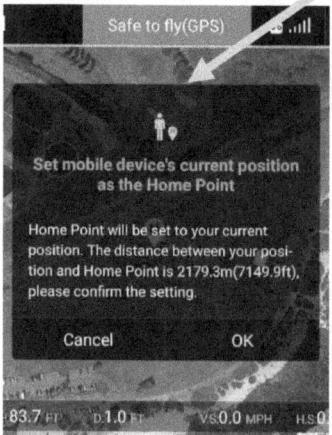

When you select the Person Icon, the above screen will display and you can set the Home Point to the location of your Mobile Device or cancel it. If the mobile device does not have a strong GPS signal, the home point cannot be set.

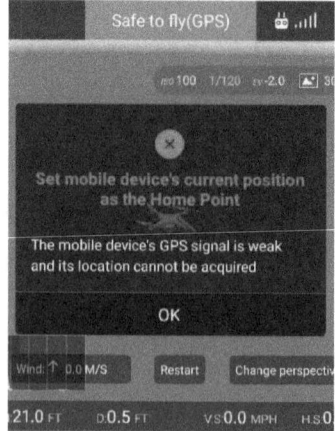

INTELLIGENT ORIENTATION CONTROL

Intelligent Orientation Control (IOC) is also known as Intelligent Navigation or Intelligent Flight mode. It allows the aircraft to fly in a controlled pattern set by the pilot. There are five modes available: Course Lock, Home Lock, Point of Interest, Follow Me, and Waypoints.

To enable it, you must do two things.

1. Toggle the S1 switch to the down position (see page 20).
2. In MC Settings under Advanced Settings, switch on "Enable Multiple Flight Mode." Please note "Enable IOC" is defunct and is not needed to enable Intelligent Orientation Control.

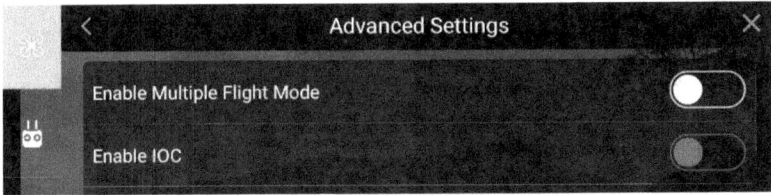

INTELLIGENT NAVIGATION MODES

Once Multiple Flight Modes / Intelligent Navigation is activated and you are in the air, the above screen should display on your mobile device. At this point, you simply select the mode you wish to fly in and follow any on-screen directions.

The aircraft must be flying to set the modes.

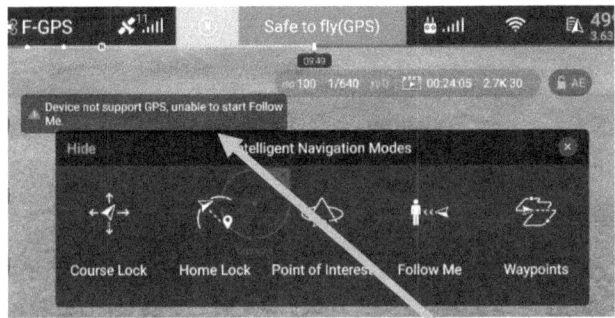

In general, the app will display notifications and warnings when you are trying to do something you can't.

Whenever you exit a flight mode, the app will ask you to confirm and then the aircraft will hover. If you wish to take control of the aircraft again, simply toggle the S1 switch to the up position.

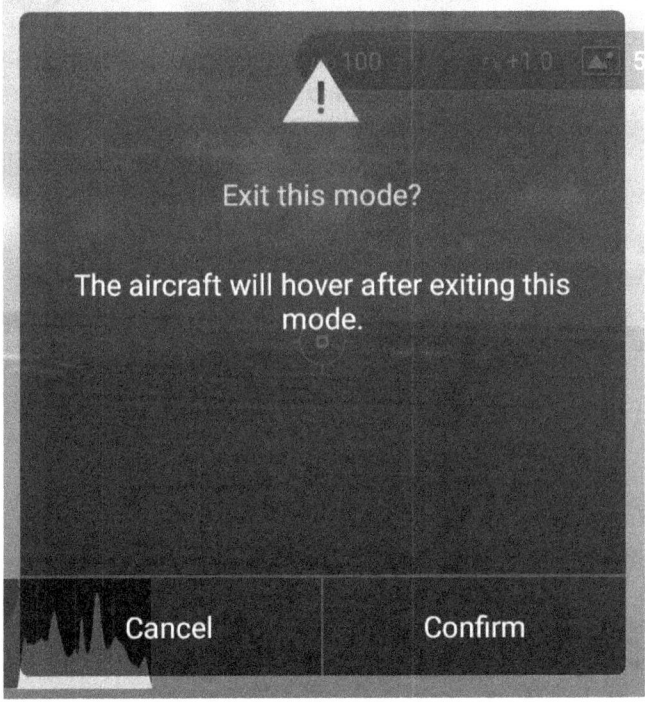

COURSE LOCK

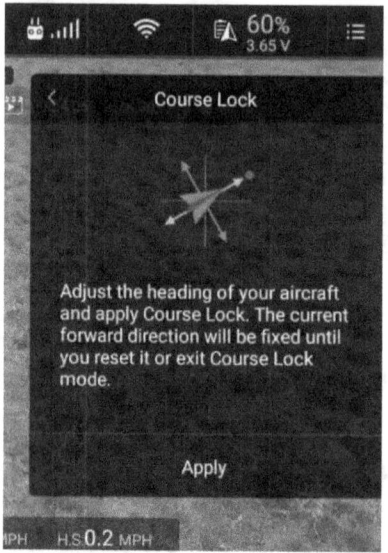

This setting locks the forward and backward direction of the aircraft on a straight flight path. For instance, if you point the aircraft to fly at a 50-degree heading, then when you push the control stick to fly forward, it will fly forward at a 50-degree heading. And when you fly backward, it will maintain that heading in the opposite direction at 230 degrees. The aircraft can still rotate and move sideways or perpendicularly, but it will be locked to the course line for forward and backward flying.

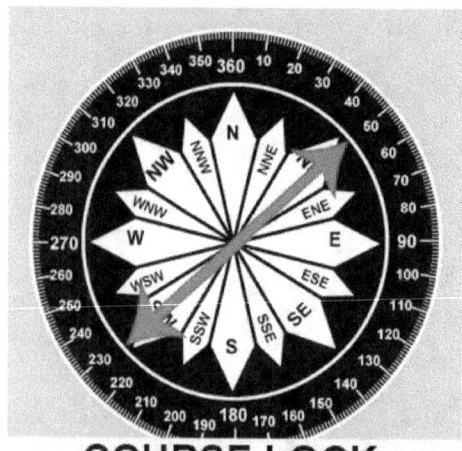

COURSE LOCK

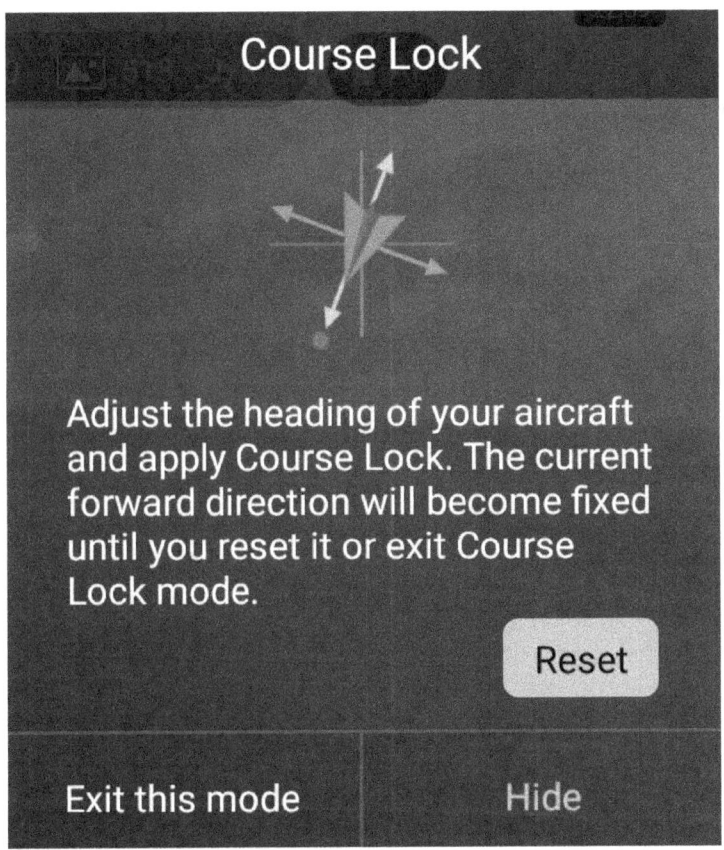

Course Lock

Adjust the heading of your aircraft and apply Course Lock. The current forward direction will become fixed until you reset it or exit Course Lock mode.

Reset

Exit this mode   Hide

To use this mode, simply point the aircraft in the direction you want it to fly and tap APPLY. Once it is set, the screen above appears. From this screen, you have the choice to Reset the direction, exit Course Lock, or hide the Course Lock screen from view.

When flying in Course Lock, all the other controls still work. It is simply the forward and backward directions that are locked.

Course Lock might be useful if you are filming a sporting event and want to lock in a flight path above the field. It might also be convenient if you are tracking a vehicle along a road and doing multiple takes.

HOME LOCK

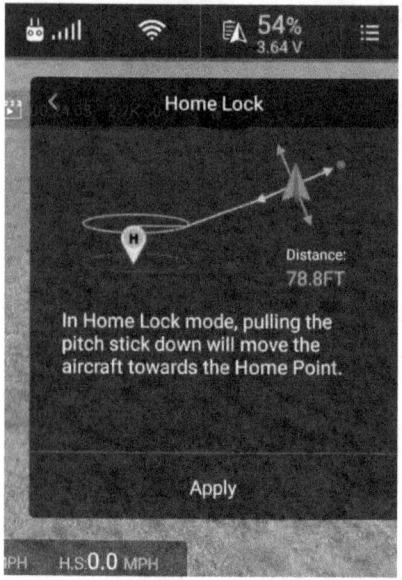

This setting locks in a linear flight path back to the Home Point. Once this is set, if you pull back on the right stick (the same stick you would use to fly backward), then no matter where the aircraft is, it will fly in a line to the Home Point. Essentially, it gives you a manual Return-To-Home functionality. To set Home Lock, the aircraft must be more than 16 feet (or 5 meters) from you. When the aircraft returns to you, it will also stop at least 16 feet from you.

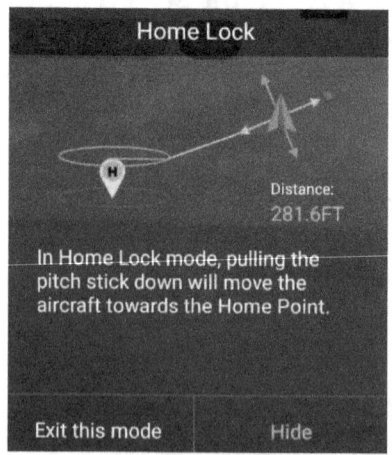

POINT OF INTEREST

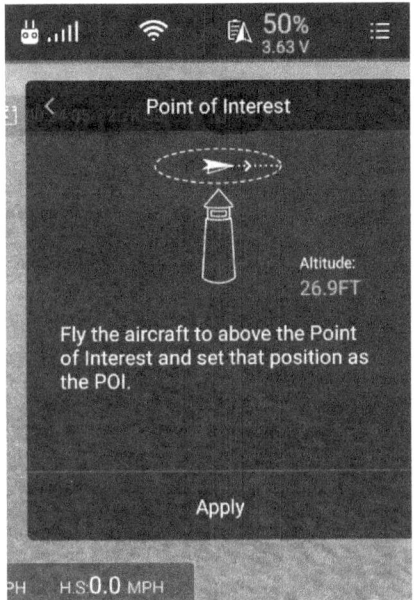

This setting lets you lock in a circular flight path around a point of interest. The first step is to hover the aircraft over the point of interest.

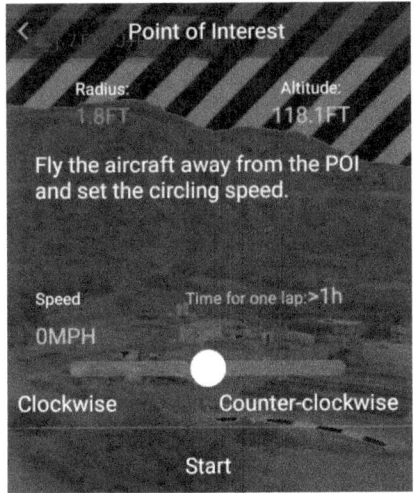

Once that is done, you fly the aircraft away from the point of interest to a shooting distance you like, then set the circling speed.

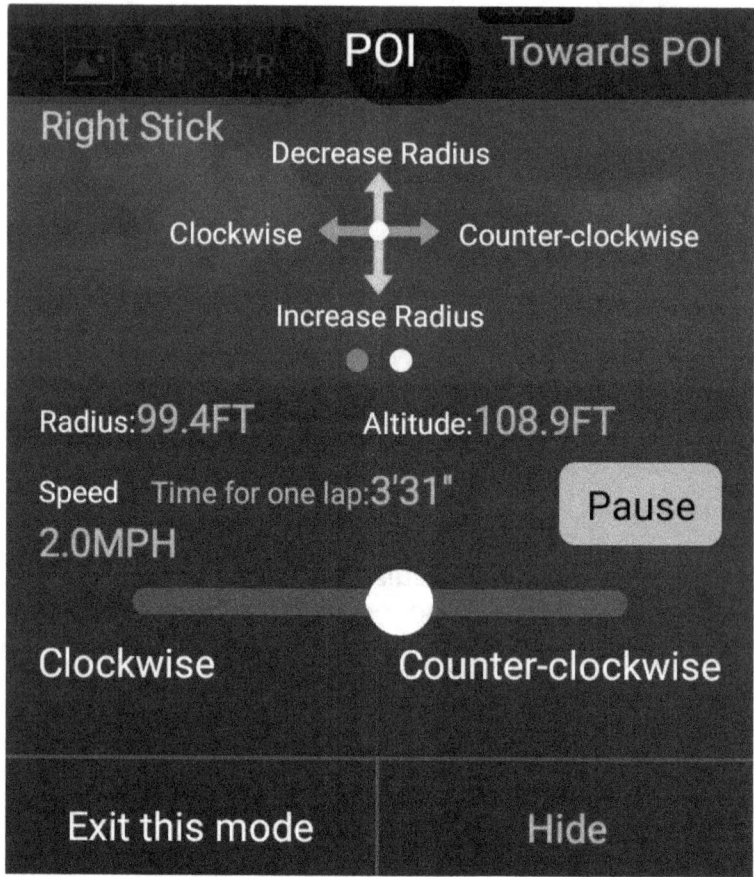

Once the aircraft begins circling, the screen above appears and gives you additional control options. From this screen, you can pause the flight, change the direction, change the radius, and exit the mode completely.

It is advisable to pause the aircraft before changing directions.

This is an amazing feature that allows you to get some very fluid and controlled circling shots that would be difficult to get manually.

FOLLOW ME MODE

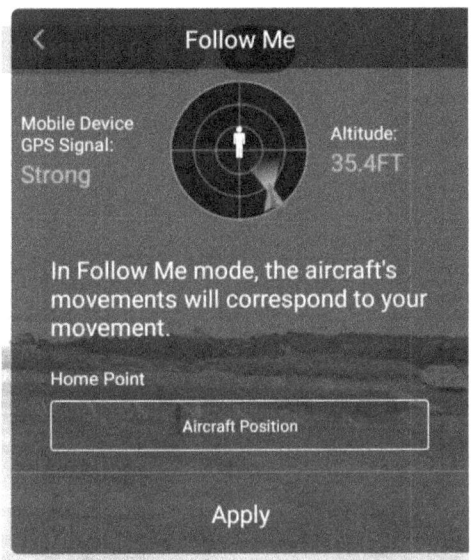

This mode allows the aircraft to track your movements. Your mobile device must have a strong GPS signal for this to work. Normally, a blue dot will appear in Map View when that is the case. From this screen, you can also set the Home Point position if you wish to change it.

WAYPOINTS

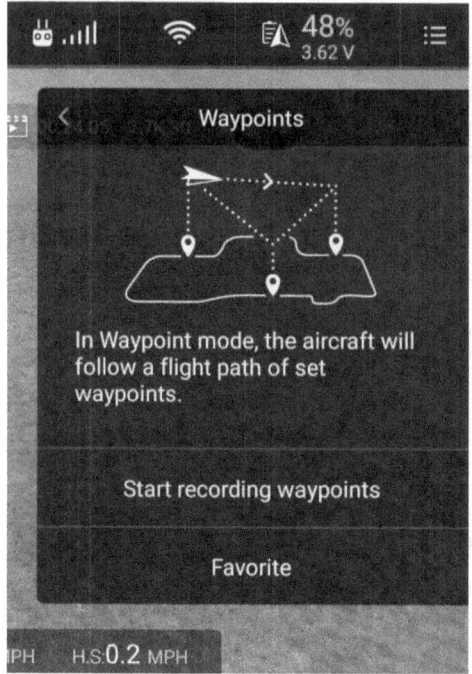

This mode will copy any flight pattern you have flown. It requires you to fly the pattern first and record the waypoints as you go. Once the points are set, then you can command the aircraft to follow the pattern.

WAYPOINT LIMITS

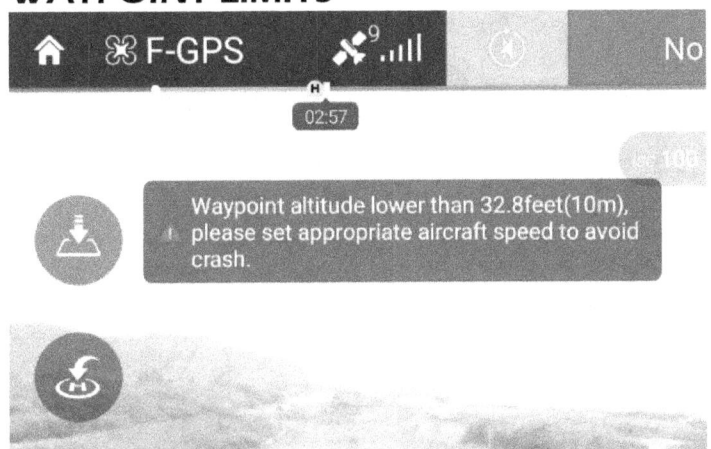

The Waypoints Mode has limits on what it can do. The app should notify you when there is an issue.

RESTRICTIONS

1. Minimum Waypoint Distance: 16.4 feet
2. Maximum Radius: 1640 feet
3. Maximum Path Length: 16,404 feet
4. If altitude lower than 32.8 feet, aircraft speed needs to be set appropriately.

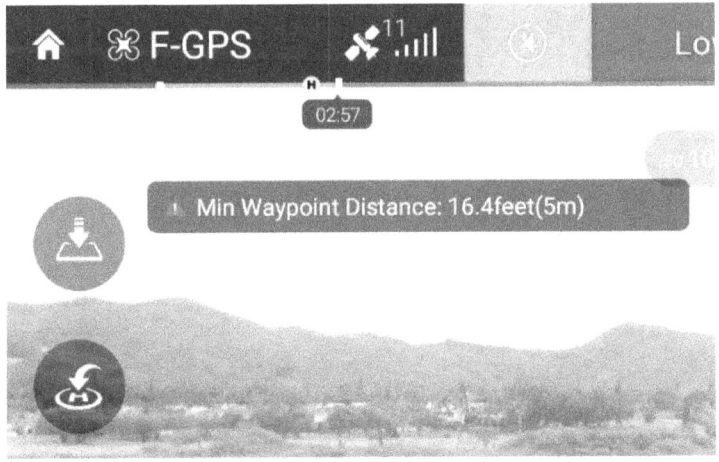

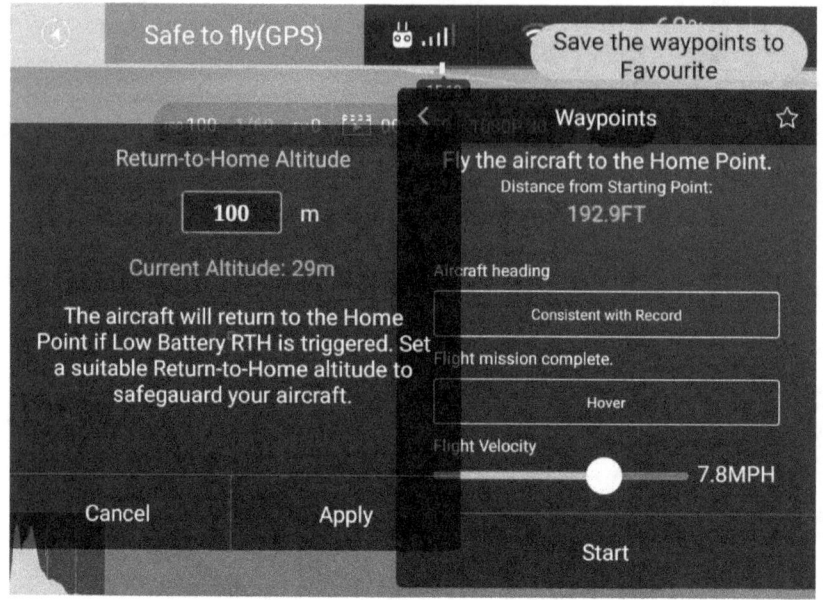

Safe to fly(GPS)

Save the waypoints to Favourite

< Waypoints ☆

Return-to-Home Altitude

Fly the aircraft to the Home Point.
Distance from Starting Point:
192.9FT

100 m

Current Altitude: 29m

Aircraft heading

The aircraft will return to the Home Point if Low Battery RTH is triggered. Set a suitable Return-to-Home altitude to safegauard your aircraft.

Consistent with Record

Flight mission complete.

Hover

Flight Velocity

7.8MPH

Cancel

Apply

Start

After the waypoints are recorded, the above screen appears.

Under Aircraft Heading, you can choose the orientation at which the aircraft flies the pattern. The choices are:

1. Consistent with Record: Flies in the same orientation it was in when the waypoints were recorded.
2. Consistent with Route: Flies facing the waypoints.
3. Free Mode: Pilot maintains control of orientation.

Under Flight Mission Complete, you can choose if the aircraft will Hover or Return-to-Home.

The app also asks you to confirm or reset the Return-to-Home Altitude. You can either leave it as is or change it.

As noted on the screen, once you are ready to start, you fly the aircraft to the Home Point and once you press Start, the aircraft will fly to the first waypoint.

Once you are in Waypoints Mode, the above screen appears. This gives you a choice to change speed, pause, or exit the mode completely.

In this mode, you can control the gimbal and also the orientation if you set it to Free Mode.

If you set the Flight Mission Complete setting to Return-to-Home (RTH), be mindful that the aircraft will initiate that procedure once the flight pattern is finished.

If the aircraft starts returning to home and you realize that is not what you want, you can cancel RTH by toggling the S1 switch back and forth a couple of times.

LANDING

There are three ways to land the aircraft: Auto-Landing, Return-To-Home, and Manual.

AUTO-LANDING

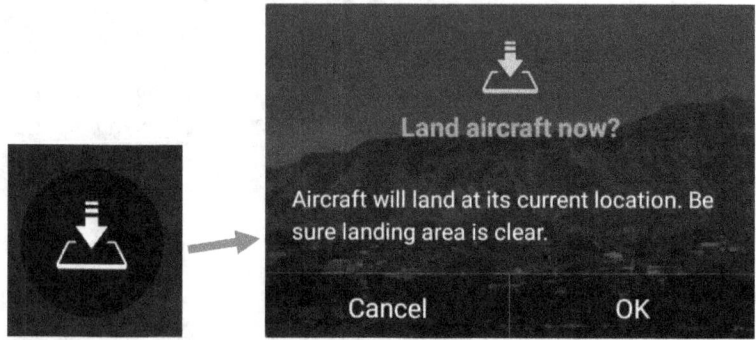

For Auto-Landing, press the Auto-Landing button, then tap OK at the prompt.

RETURN-TO-HOME

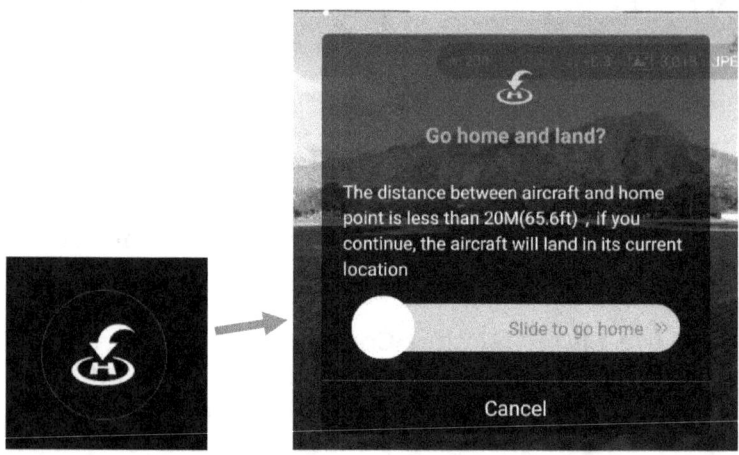

For Return-To-Home (RTH), press the RTH button, then slide the Switch to confirm. This initiates the RTH procedure. If the aircraft is already within 20 meters or 65.6 feet of the Home Point, it will automatically land in its current position.

MANUAL LANDING

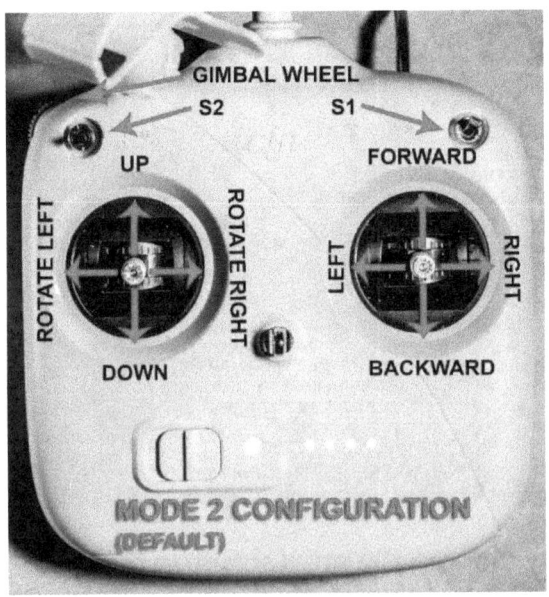

To land the aircraft manually, use the left stick and pull the stick toward you. Bring the aircraft down very slowly until it is hovering just inches above the ground. Once the aircraft is stable in that position, gently finish bringing it all the way down to the ground. Once it touches the ground, hold the stick all the way back until the propellers stop. With practice, you should be able to land the aircraft softly.

For both take-offs and landings, it is advisable to find a level surface that is free from dust, dirt, and debris. Usually, low-cut grass makes for a perfect place to land. Do not do hand-grab landings or touch the aircraft at any time the propellers are spinning.

The Combination Stick Control (CSC) or two-stick method of landing the aircraft is not recommended. I have experienced first-hand that when a landing is made that way, there is a spike in propeller speed, which can cause the aircraft to tip over.

If you do not feel comfortable landing the aircraft manually, then use the Auto-Landing feature instead. As in general aviation, landing takes the most skill.

MAP VIEW

Activate Map View by tapping the small screen in the lower left corner. Map View can be especially helpful if you happen to lose sight of the aircraft and are trying to navigate back home.

CHOICE OF VIEW

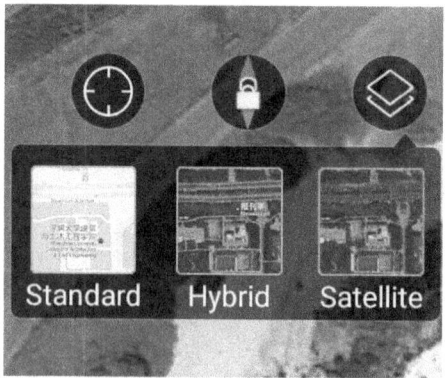

Map View offers three views, which can be selected by tapping the icon in the upper right corner.

SATELLITE: An aerial view with no text or markers.
HYBRID: The names of streets, areas, landmarks, and markers are superimposed on an aerial view.
STANDARD: A traditional map view with no aerial imagery.

COMPASS LOCK

If you tap the Compass Icon, it unlocks the compass and rotates the view as a free-spinning compass.

If you wish to lock it, simply tap the icon again.

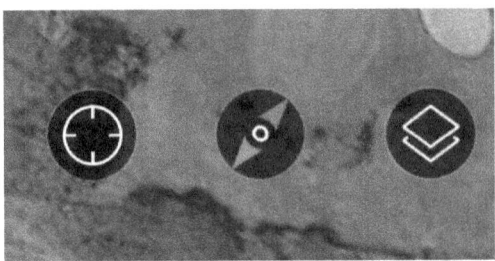

MAP CACHE

If you plan to fly the aircraft and want to use Map View but will be using a mobile device that does not have active cell service, then you can cache the map. This means you can load the map into the mobile device's memory and have it available for reference when you fly. If you don't cache the map, then it will be blank. To cache the map, follow these steps.

1. Turn on your mobile device.
2. Open the DJI GO app
3. Enter Camera View
4. Open Map View
5. Swipe through the map until you have fully viewed the entire area where you plan to fly.

Fully viewing the map in your mobile device loads it into the cache and it will then be available for viewing even if you don't have cell service. The aircraft and remote do not need to be on to cache the map.

CENTER FUNCTION

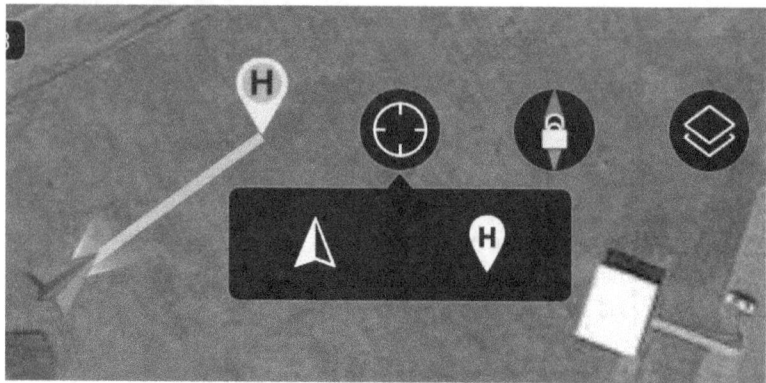

The Center Icon will position either the Aircraft or the Home Point Icon to the center of the Map View screen. Also, notice that the green beam in front of the aircraft highlights the direction it is flying in.

THE BLUE DOT

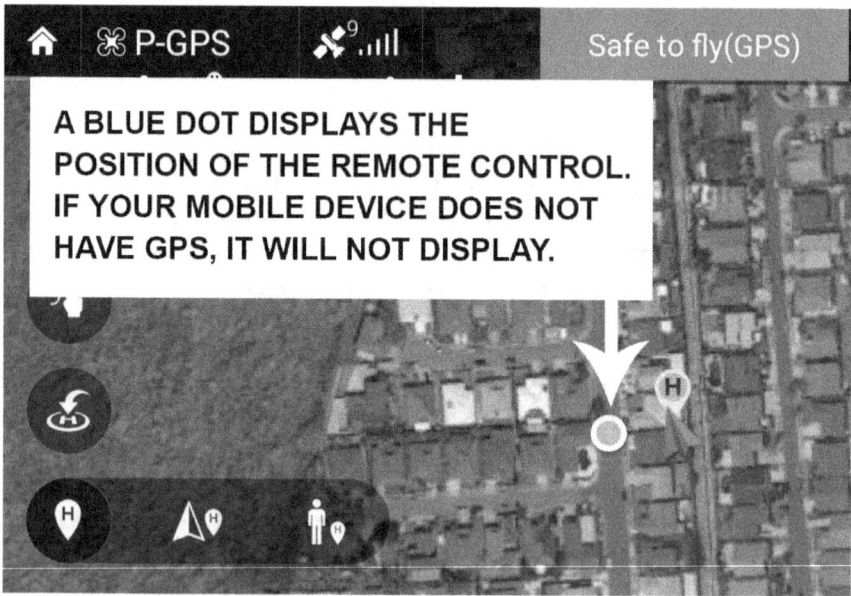

If your mobile device has GPS, then you should see a blue dot, which represents the position of the remote control. If you do not have GPS, then the blue dot will not appear. If the mobile device acquires GPS through a Wi-Fi, the dot can also appear.

MC SETTINGS

MC Settings can be accessed from the Main Screen in one of two locations. On the top left, tap the MC Settings icon or on the top right, tap the General Settings icon.

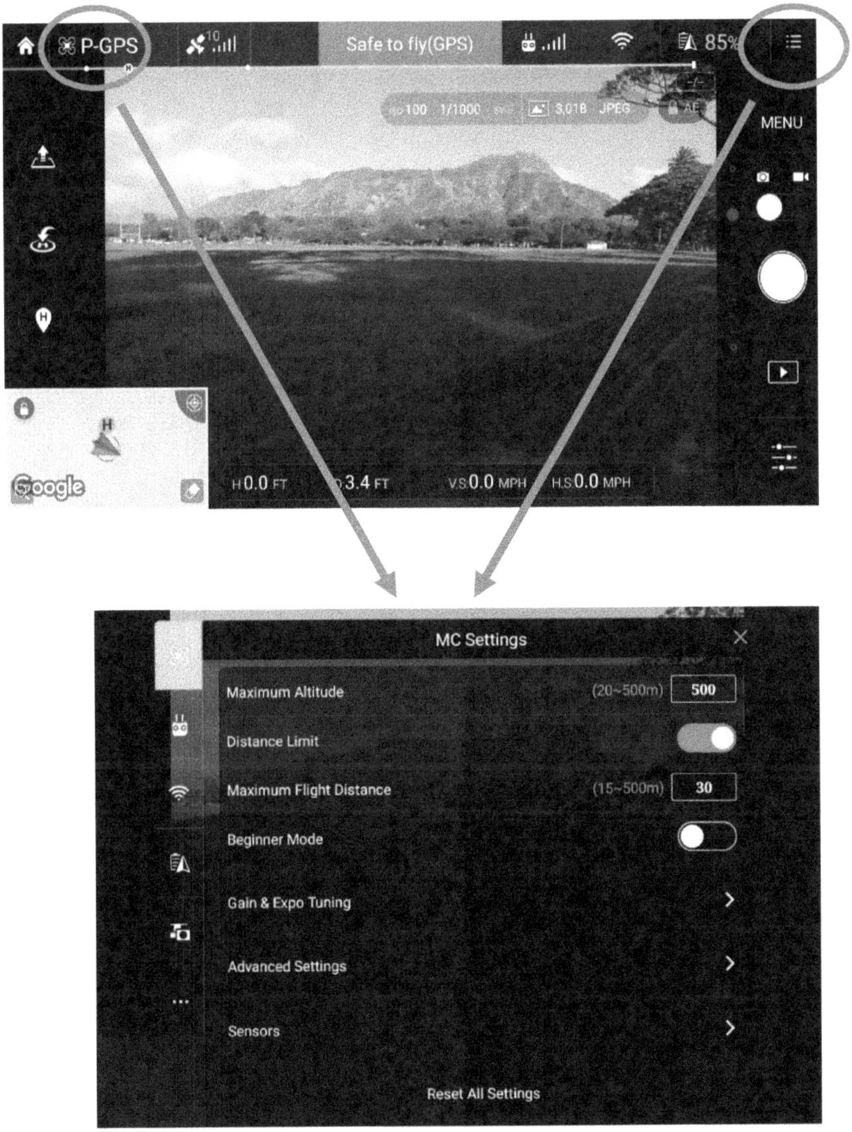

MC Settings

Maximum Altitude   (20~500m) 500

Distance Limit

Maximum Flight Distance   (15~500m) 30

Beginner Mode

Gain & Expo Tuning   >

Advanced Settings   >

Sensors   >

Reset All Settings

MAIN CONTROLLER SETTINGS
MENU OPTIONS AT GLANCE

FIRST LEVEL	SECOND LEVEL	THIRD LEVEL
MAX ALTITUDE		
DISTANCE LIMIT		
MAX FLIGHT DISTANCE		
BEGINNER MODE		
GAIN & EXPO TUNING >		
	EXP	
	THROTTLE	
	RUDDER	
	FORWARD	
	SENSITIVITY	
	ATTITUDE	
	BRAKE	
	YAW ENDPOINT	
	GAIN >	
		BASIC GAIN
		PITCH
		ROLL
		YAW
		VERTICAL
ADVANCED SETTINGS >		
	ENABLE MULTIPLE FLIGHT MODES	
	ENABLE IOC	
	RESET IOC	
	FAIL SAFE MODE >	
		RETURN ALTITUDE
	RC SIGNAL LOST >	
		RETURN-TO-HOME
		LANDING
		HOVER
		ENTER FLIGHT DATA
		TURN ON ARM'S LEDS
SENSORS >		
	GYROSCOPE	
	ACCELERATION	
	COMPASS	
	IMU CALIBRATION	
	RESET ALL SETTINGS	

MC SETTINGS (HOME PAGE)

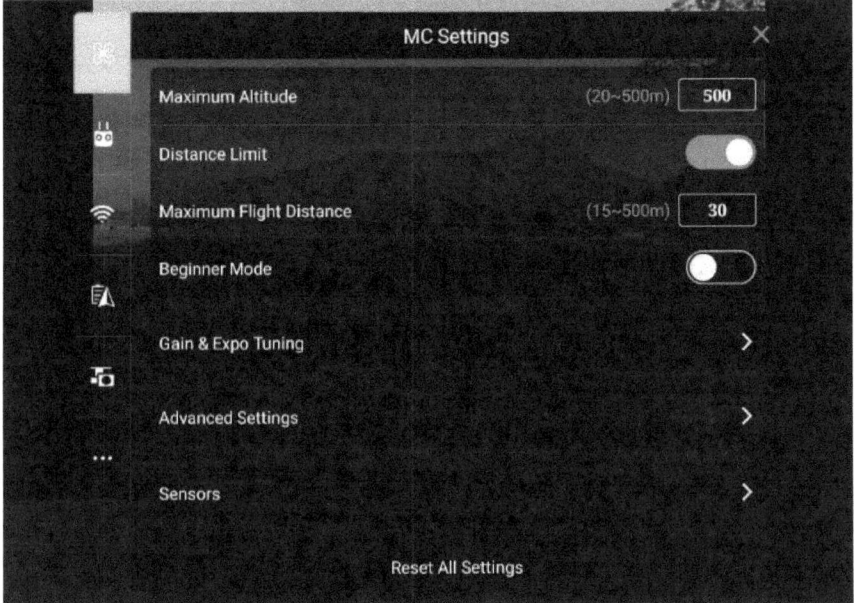

On the MC Settings Home Page, there are four settings that can be adjusted. The remaining options drill down to other menus.

MAXIMUM ALTITUDE: Sets a maximum height or ceiling for the aircraft's operation. In the United States, the Federal Aviation Administration states this should be no higher than 400 feet. The maximum can be set between 20 - 500 meters (65 – 1,640 feet).

DISTANCE LIMIT: Enables the distance limit function. If no distance limit is set, then the distance limit is influenced by the strength of the remote control signal.

MAXIMUM FLIGHT DISTANCE: Sets a distance limit on how far the aircraft can fly. The maximum can be set between 15 - 500 meters (49 – 1,640 feet).

BEGINNER MODE: Imposes altitude and distance limits of 100 feet or 30 meters. This provides a measure of safety and reassurance for beginning pilots. When it is turned off, the altitude and distance limits can then be customized. This mode can be turned off while the aircraft is in flight.

GAIN & EXPO TUNING

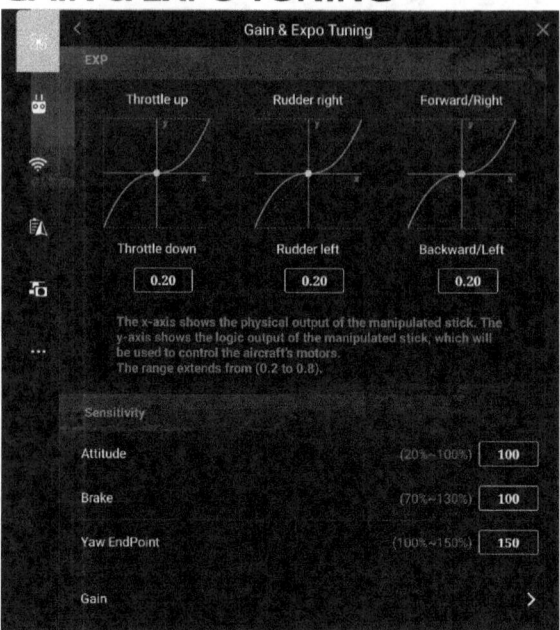

Exponential Settings control how aggressively the aircraft will respond to the movement of the control sticks on the remote controller. The range extends from .20 to .80. The higher the number, the more responsive the aircraft is to control stick movement. A lower number means the aircraft will react slowly and sluggishly. (The definitions below assume Mode 2 is the configuration on the remote controller.)

THROTTLE UP/DOWN: Controls the responsiveness of the aircraft in reaction to throttle stick movement. The throttle controls the up-and-down movement of the aircraft. On the remote, this is pushing the left stick forward or back.

RUDDER RIGHT/LEFT (YAW): Controls the responsiveness of the aircraft in reaction to rudder stick movement. The rudder controls the rotation or spin of the aircraft. On the remote, this is pushing the left stick side to side.

FORWARD/BACKWARD & LEFT/RIGHT: Controls the responsiveness of the aircraft in reaction to the right control stick. On the remote, this stick controls forward & backward and left & right movement.

GAIN & EXPO TUNING (CONTINUED)

Sensitivity Settings control how responsive the aircraft is to user input. For all these settings, a higher percentage means more responsiveness or greater reaction, and a lower percentage means less responsiveness or less reaction. Caution should also be used when adjusting these settings. If the controls become too soft or sluggish, it might be more difficult to control the aircraft.

ATTITUDE: Sets the overall responsiveness or aggressiveness of the aircraft.

BRAKE: Controls how fast the aircraft comes to a stop once you let go of the control sticks or push them to the center position.

YAW ENDPOINT: Controls the rate at which the aircraft rotates or spins. The higher the number, the faster the rotation.

GAIN: Enters a submenu.

GAIN SETTINGS

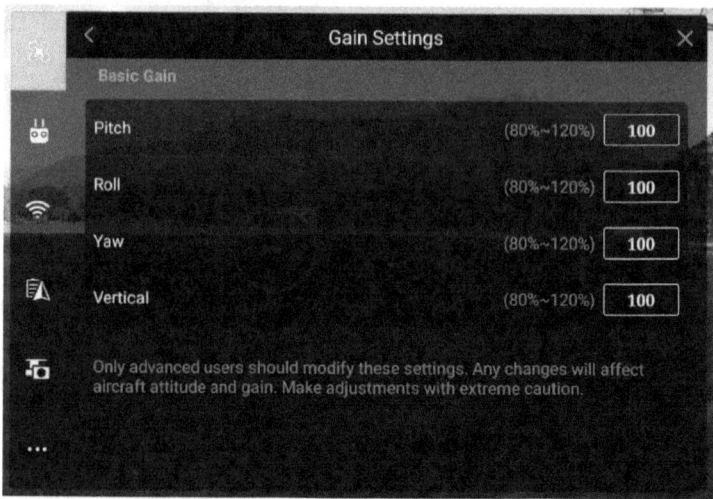

Gain Settings control how the aircraft responds to external forces acting upon it such as wind. For all the Gain Settings, a lower percentage makes the aircraft less responsive; a higher number makes it more responsive. DJI recommends that only advanced users change these settings from the default. For instance, if the settings are adjusted low, then the aircraft might have difficulty recovering position from a strong gust of wind. Adjust with caution.

PITCH: Sets the responsiveness for forward and backward movement.

ROLL: Sets the responsiveness for sideways movement, that is, left to right or right to left.

YAW: Sets the responsiveness for rotating or spinning.

VERTICAL: Sets the responsiveness for movement up and down.

By default, all the settings are at 100%.

If you choose to alter these settings, it is recommended that you only change one setting at a time and use small adjustments to start, for instance, 5-10%. You should test the changes on a calm day in a safe, open area.

ADVANCED SETTINGS

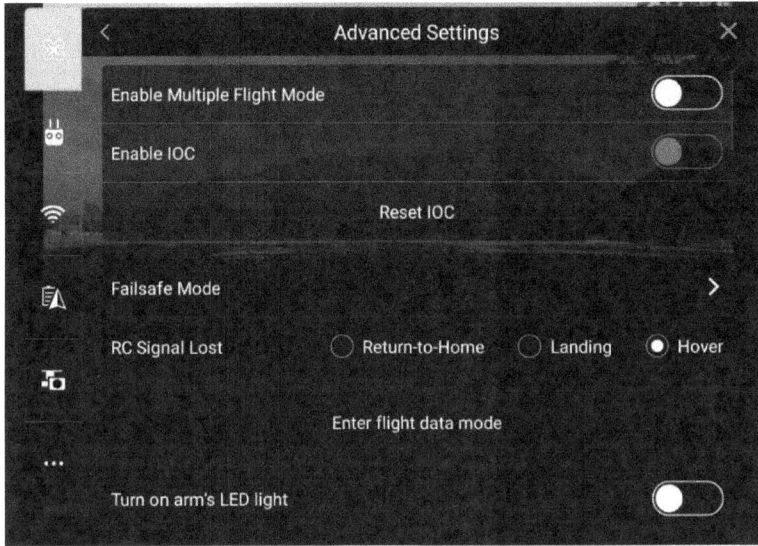

ENABLE MULTIPLE FLIGHT MODE: This switch must be enabled or turned on to fly in Intelligent Navigation or IOC mode.

ENABLE IOC: This setting is defunct or not applicable.

FAIL SAFE MODE: This takes you to the screen where you can set your Return-to-Home Altitude.

RC SIGNAL LOST: Controls what the aircraft does in the event the aircraft loses the signal from the remote control.

ENTER FLIGHT DATA MODE: Allows you to extract .dat files from the aircraft. These files contain detailed flight information that might be useful in understanding what happened during a particular flight. To view the .dat files, you can go to a log viewer website such as the one at mapsmadeeasy.com.
URL: http://support.dronesmadeeasy.com/hc/en-us/articles/206171443

TURN ON ARM'S LED LIGHT: Turns on the red LED lights on the front of the aircraft. Useful when flying by sight.

RETURN-TO-HOME ALTITUDE

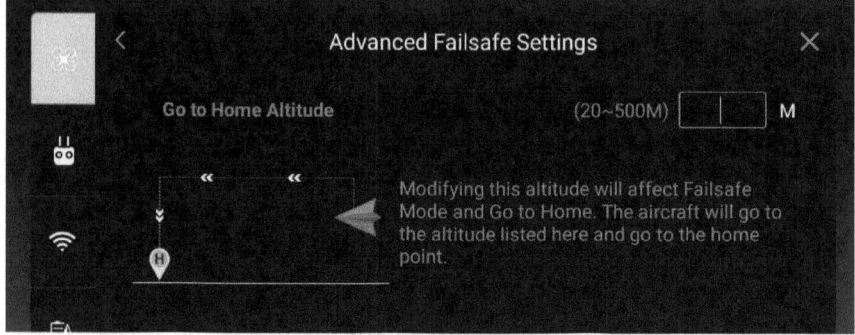

This is an extremely important setting to check before every flight. At any time that the Return-to-Home procedure is initiated, then the aircraft will automatically ascend to an altitude of 65 feet before returning to the Home Point unless you have set a different return altitude. If there are any obstacles between the aircraft and the home point that are taller than 65 feet, then the aircraft might crash into them.

No matter how excited you are to start flying, always take your time and go through the Preflight Checklist, which includes double-checking your Return-to-Home altitude.

You can cancel the Return-to-Home procedure by toggling the S1 switch back and forth a couple of times. Toggling the S2 switch on the remote control initiates the Return-to-Home procedure. It might be helpful to remember a rhyme like this:

S1 CANCEL WHAT'S DONE
S2 SENDS IT TO YOU

SENSORS

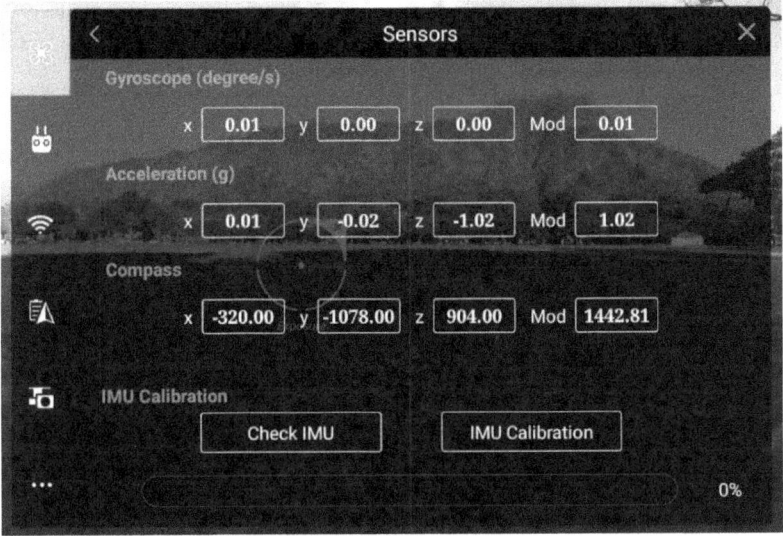

This screen provides real-time data related to the aircraft's sensors and may indicate a need for calibration, a problem with magnetic interference, or an issue with the sensors. If the sensors are giving unusual readings, you should evaluate if it is safe to fly. It is a good practice to note the Mod Values after each calibration and to check them before each flight to see if they are deviating from the established base values. If they are, resolve the issue before flying. A status message or light sequence may also alert you. [Gyroscopes and accelerometers comprise the Inertial Measurement Unit (IMU).]

GYROSCOPES: Measure angular velocity and orientation. The Mod Value is typically at or close to 0.00.

ACCELEROMETERS: Measure acceleration and momentum. The Mod Value is typically at or close to 1.00.

COMPASS (MAGNETOMETER): Measures direction. This Mod Value can vary significantly. An acceptable Mod Value in most places is between 1,400 and 1,600; however, compass readings can vary based on your location and latitude, so it is not practical to define a universally accepted Mod Value range. The best suggestion is to do a proper compass calibration and note the *normal* range for your area.

IMU CALIBRATION

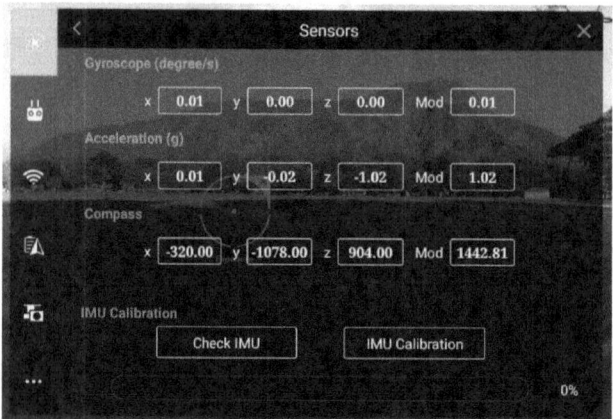

If you tap on Check IMU, it will advise you if the IMU needs calibration. If it does not, you will receive the notice as shown below.

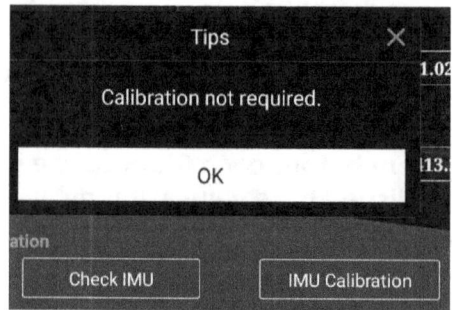

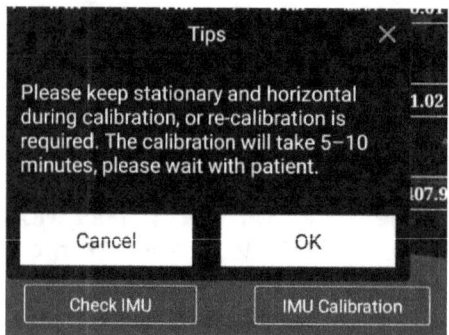

If you tap on IMU Calibration, it will begin the recalibration process. Follow the on-screen directions to proceed.

OTHER

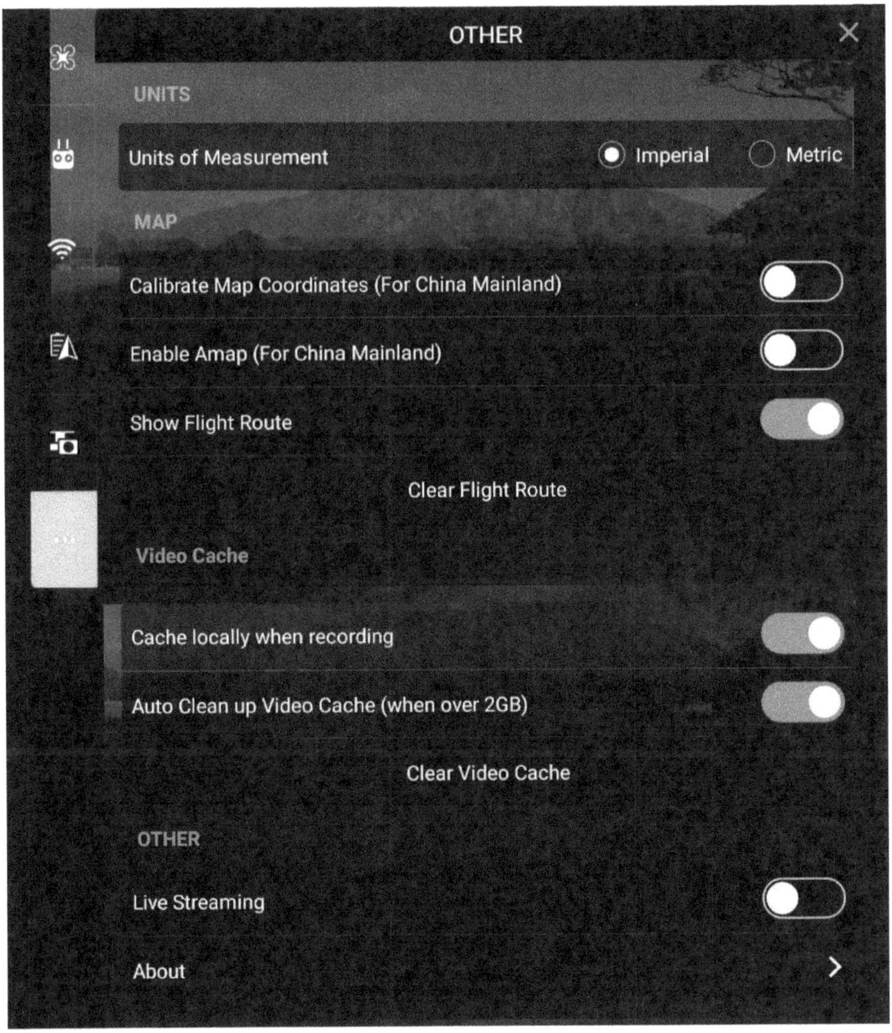

OTHER   ✕

UNITS

Units of Measurement   ● Imperial   ○ Metric

MAP

Calibrate Map Coordinates (For China Mainland)

Enable Amap (For China Mainland)

Show Flight Route

Clear Flight Route

Video Cache

Cache locally when recording

Auto Clean up Video Cache (when over 2GB)

Clear Video Cache

OTHER

Live Streaming

About   ›

UNITS OF MEASUREMENT: Set to Imperial or Metric standards.

CALIBRATE MAP COORDINATES: Adjusts map coordinates to mainland China. Unnecessary elsewhere.

ENABLE AMAP: A mapping system for use in mainland China only. Unnecessary elsewhere.

SHOW FLIGHT ROUTE: Shows the flight route of the aircraft.

CLEAR FLIGHT ROUTE: Tap to erase flight route.

CACHE LOCALLY WHEN RECORDING: Enables the aircraft's camera to record to the connected mobile device. If disabled, it will only record to the camera's SD card. Disabling it also frees memory on the mobile device.

AUTO CLEAN UP VIDEO CACHE: Automatically clears the video cache on the mobile device once it exceeds 2 Gigabytes.

LIVE STREAMING: This is supposed to enable live streaming to sites such as You Tube; however, for the Standard model, it does not work.

CLEAR VIDEO CACHE: Tap to delete video files in the cache.

ABOUT

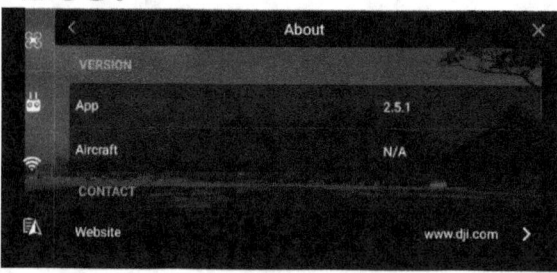

APP: Displays the current version of the GO app.

AIRCRAFT: Defunct setting.

WEBSITE: Links to the DJI website.

PREFLIGHT CHECKLIST

- Aircraft battery, remote, and mobile device are fully charged.
- Check the propellers for tightness.
- Inspect the aircraft for any damage.
- Remove the gimbal lock if one is attached.
- Check the lens and clean if necessary.
- Make sure the SD card is in the camera.
- Install ND filter(s). [A light meter can confirm filter(s) needed.] [1]
- Turn on the remote control.
- Turn on the aircraft.
- Turn on the mobile device. [2]
- Confirm latest firmware is installed.
- Verify camera settings (frame rate, ISO, shutter speed, etc.)
- Double-check exposure with histogram and EV meter.
- Check IMU and sensor readings.
- Calibrate the compass if needed.
- Note wind direction and the height of any obstacles. [3]
- Confirm the Return-To-Home altitude is set appropriately.
- Confirm home point is set to the right location.
- Check SD card is formatted or has ample space for recording.
- Check antenna is pointed up and parallel to the craft.
- Check S1 switch for Flight Mode. (Consider P-Mode to start.)
- Confirm area is safe for flying and landing.
- Confirm aircraft lights are flashing as safe to fly.
- Start motors.
- Start video recording.[4]
- Throttle up.
- Hover initially and check sticks for operation.
- Keep the aircraft in line of sight at all times.
- Cleared for flight.

NOTES
1. Shooting video on a sunny day requires ND filters. Filming at dusk, dawn, or in low light may not. ND filters are not required for taking photos.
2. In direct sunlight, you need shade for your mobile device to reduce glare.
3. Do not fly in high winds or other adverse conditions.
4. Be sure to stop the video recording before you turn off the aircraft.

REGULATIONS

As of December 21, 2015, the Federal Aviation Administration (FAA) passed a rule mandating the registration of all unmanned aircraft systems or drones weighing more than .55 and less than 55 pounds. The registration is done online, costs $5, and is good for three years. According to the FAA, failure to register your drone can result in civil fines up to $27,500 and criminal penalties, which include fines up to $250,000 and three years in prison.

In addition, drones may only be used for recreational, nonprofit activities. If you plan to use the drone for commercial purposes, then you need to file for an exemption with the FAA and meet other rather burdensome requirements such as having a pilot's license.

The law governing the use of drones is evolving, and the FAA will eventually release revisions that hopefully make more practical sense than the current ones. But either way, it is important to keep informed and register.

RC SETTINGS

REMOTE CONTROL SETTINGS

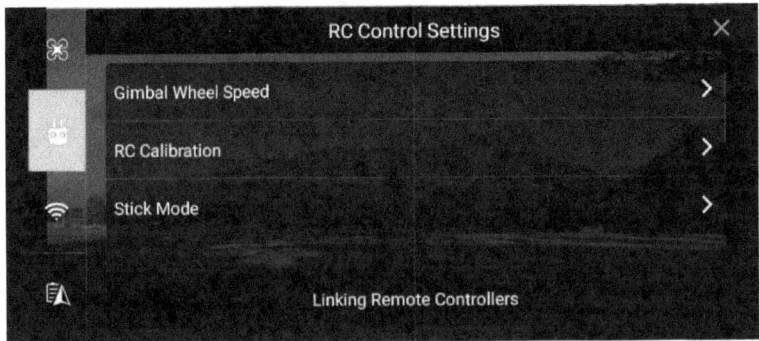

This screen allows to navigate to one of three submenus and also allows you to initiate the procedure for linking to a remote controller.

GIMBAL WHEEL SPEED

Controls the rate of gimbal movement in response to the gimbal wheel. It adjusts in increments of ten from 0 to 100. The higher the number, the faster the gimbal moves. When set to a low number such as ten, it can take the gimbal more than two minutes to tilt all the way up or down. In terms of functionality, it serves a purpose similar to gimbal pitch, which also controls the speed of the gimbal's movement. Since Gimbal Pitch adjusts in increments of one, it is considered to offer a finer degree of control than Gimbal Wheel Speed.

RC CALIBRATION

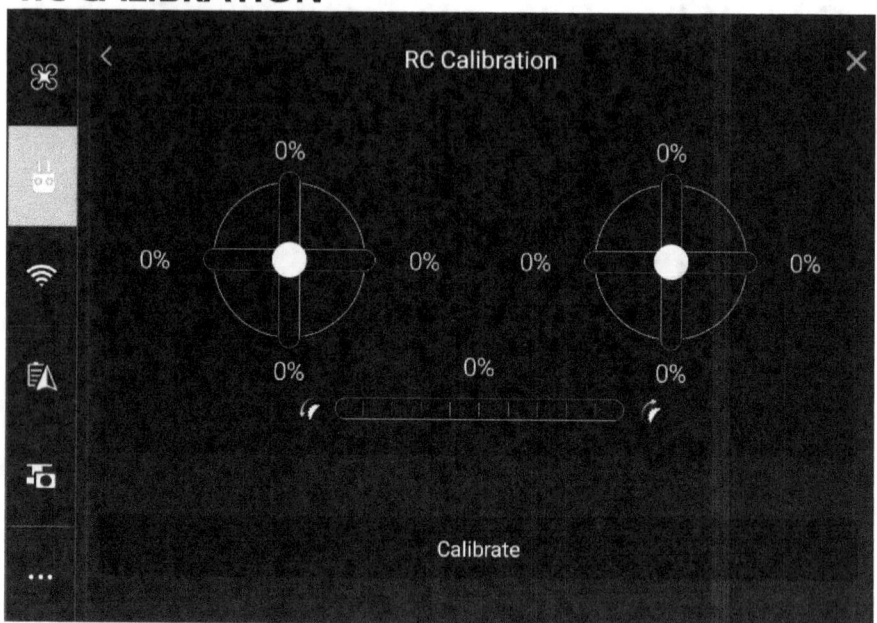

RC Calibration can be done when the remote controller is not working properly or you have done the linking procedure but the remote controller's red light stays on and you hear a continuous beeping.

To do the actual calibration, make sure the aircraft is off, then turn on the remote controller. Navigate to the RC Calibration screen on the GO app and tap on the Calibrate button. From there, move the sticks and the dial according to the on-screen instructions. Once you have completed that process, tap Finish, and the remote should be properly working. If it is not, then you can either try the procedure again or contact DJI Support for additional assistance.

MASTER STICK MODE

The active mode is marked with the black check.

Master Stick Mode lets you change the location of control stick functions. For instance, if you prefer to have Forward & Backward and Left & Right controlled by the left stick and not the right stick, then you would switch from Mode 2 to Mode 3.

There are three preset configurations to choose from. By default, the remote controller is set to Mode 2. To change the mode, simply tap on the mode you want, then confirm the change.

You can also set up a Custom configuration. To do that, you simply tap on the Custom mode, then click and drag the control functions to where you want them.

You should exercise caution when changing control stick functions.

Once you practice with and become familiar with a particular control stick configuration, it can be confusing and disorienting to modify that configuration.

REMOTE CONTROLLER

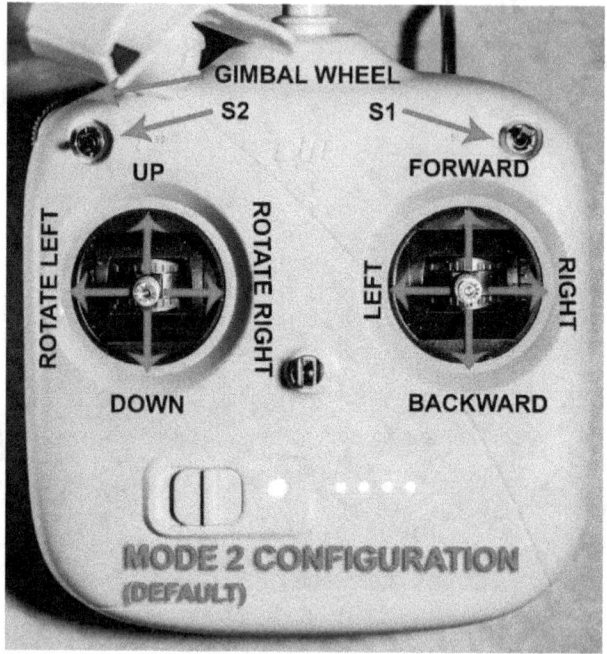

The basic controls are noted in the picture above. Most are self-explanatory except switches S1 and S2.

S1 SWITCH

1. When the aircraft is returning to home in Failsafe Mode, toggling the switch multiple times cancels the Return-to-Home protocol.
2. Toggling the switch back and forth at least 3 times initiates Compass Calibration.
3. Sets the Flight Mode you are in. (see page 20)

S2 SWITCH

1. Toggling the switch at least 2 times initiates the Return-to-Home protocol.
2. The switch is used with gimbal wheel when linking to the Aircraft and resetting the Wi-Fi password.

S1 CANCELS WHAT'S DONE
S2 SENDS IT TO YOU

RETURN-TO-HOME

There are four return-to-home functions: Smart, Low Battery, Critically Low Battery, and Failsafe.

The return-to-home function requires:

1. A properly-recorded home point
2. A strong GPS signal.

If it is missing either one of these things, it will not work.

During all return-to-home functions, the aircraft will ascend to 65 feet (unless set otherwise) and will land within 65 feet of the home point. This is why it is important to take off from a wide open, unpopulated area. Also, the Return-to-Home altitude can be adjusted under the GO app.
[see MC SETTINGS>ADVANCED>FAILSAFE MODE}

SMART RETURN-TO-HOME

You can initiate Return-to-Home manually by tapping the Return-to-Home button. Once you do that, the confirmation screen below appears. Slide the button to initiate.

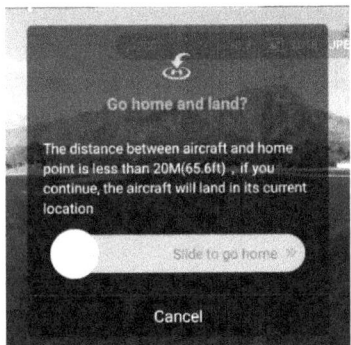

LOW BATTERY
RETURN-TO-HOME

There are two types of low battery returns.

The first is the low battery Return-to-Home that is triggered automatically when the Battery Level indicator reaches the yellow zone or reaches a preset limit, usually 30%. The aircraft will prompt you to Return-to-Home and if no action is taken within 10 seconds, the aircraft will ascend to 65 feet (unless set otherwise), then starts heading to the Home Point and will land within 65 feet of it.

If you wish to regain control of the aircraft, you can do so by toggling the S1 switch on the controller multiple times or pressing the RTH button again.

CRITICALLY LOW BATTERY
RETURN-TO-HOME

The second is a critically low battery Return-to-Home that is triggered automatically when the Battery Level indicator reaches the red zone on the Battery Level indicator or a preset limit, usually 10%. This is often bad news and means the aircraft will land wherever it is. This setting cannot be canceled, so unless the aircraft is above an open unpopulated area, it will be landing somewhere it is probably not meant to. *This is why you do not want the battery to ever reach a critical level.*

FAILSAFE RETURN-TO-HOME

The last type of Return-to-Home is Failsafe. This occurs when the aircraft has lost contact with the remote controller for more than three seconds. Like the others, it requires a recorded home point *and* a strong GPS signal. Once this mode is activated, the aircraft will ascend to 65 feet (or any custom altitude you have previously set), return to within 65 feet of the home point, hover for 15 seconds, then land. If the remote control signal is restored, you can regain control of the aircraft by toggling the S1 switch multiple times.

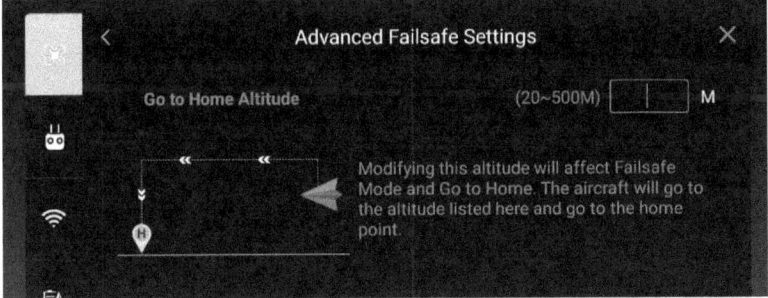

It is extremely important to make sure your Go-to-Home altitude is high enough to avoid any potential obstacles and that you are flying from a place that gives you ample room for an emergency landing. And remember that aircraft will not land at the exact Home Point but within 65 feet of it.

SHUTTER SPEED, ISO, & EXPOSURE MODE

Shutter Speed, ISO, and the Exposure Mode settings can be accessed by tapping the Sliders Icon in the lower right corner.

When the screen opens, tap the top button to select Auto-Exposure or Manual Mode.

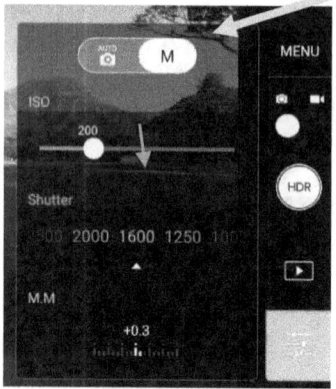

If you select Auto-Exposure, then Shutter Speed and ISO cannot be adjusted individually. If you choose Manual Mode, you retain full control over those settings.

For photos, either Manual or Auto-Exposure can be acceptable, but for video, you should always choose Manual Mode. For video, if you choose Auto-Exposure, the system will automatically adjust the shutter speed and ISO, which can result in extreme settings that often result in poor video quality.

SHUTTER SPEED

The electronic shutter has a range from 8 seconds to $1/8000^{th}$ of a second.

For photography, the shutter speed can be adjusted manually or automatically to the extremes with few, if any, concerns.

For video, however, the shutter speed should be set manually and should be double the frame rate. For instance, if the frame rate is 30, then the shutter speed should be 60.

ISO

ISO refers to the sensitivity of the sensor as a result of signal amplification; however, when the signal is amplified, digital noise can be created and significantly degrade the image.

For photos, the ISO ranges from 100 to 1,600, and for video, it ranges from 100 to 3,200.

If at all possible, it is recommended that you keep the ISO as low as possible. This will help ensure that you get a quality image with minimal noise and grain. High ISO settings usually result in an unacceptable level of grain and noise.

E.V. COMPENSATION

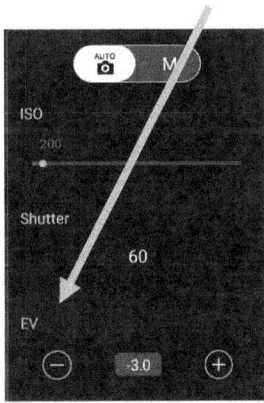

Exposure Value Compensation lets you darken or brighten an image while in Auto-Exposure Mode. This works by adjusting the ISO and/or shutter speed. Tapping the Minus Sign darkens the image while tapping the Plus Sign brightens it.

MANUAL MODE (M.M.)

In Manual Mode, you can set the camera's exposure manually by adjusting the ISO and Shutter Speed. Manual Mode also provides an Exposure Meter that lets you know how many stops you are above or below a proper exposure.

The meter is scaled in thirds, so .3 would be 1/3 of a stop, .6 would be 2/3 of a stop, and 1 would be a full stop. The meter only has a range from -2 to +2 stops.

Theoretically, if the meter is at 0, then the image should be properly exposed or relatively close.

For video, it is not a good practice to increase ISO or change the shutter speed in order to obtain a proper exposure.

For underexposure with video, it is best to wait until external lighting conditions become sufficient for a proper exposure.

For overexposure with video, it is best to apply ND filters. These methods are not necessarily convenient, but they will result in higher-quality video.

For photography, there are generally no major problems with adjusting the shutter speed to get a proper exposure.

You should only increase ISO as a last resort. Increasing it runs the risk of introducing digital noise or grain into the footage.

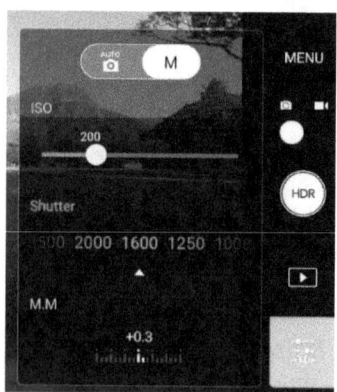

SELECTIVE AUTO-EXPOSURE

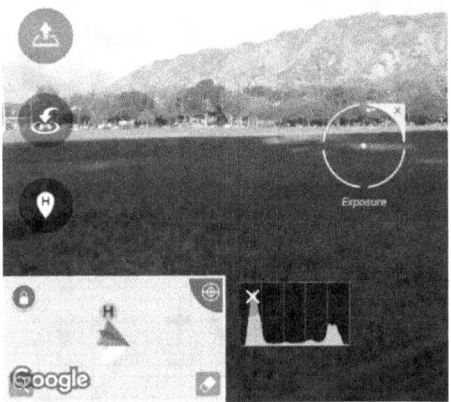

If the camera is set to Auto-Exposure Mode, when you touch anywhere on the image, the Selective Auto-Exposure Control will appear. This will bring that area of the image into proper exposure but may also blow out or darken other areas as well. If you are in Manual Mode, Selective Auto-Exposure will not appear.

APERTURE

The camera has a wide-angle lens of 20 millimeters that is focused to infinity and has a fixed aperture of 2.8. For shooting video, the lens requires the use of ND filters in order to control the amount of light coming into the camera. Please note that you do not need ND filters for photos, only video.

For video, if the shutter speed is increased to control the light, then the footage is likely to appear unnatural. Without ND filters, the only times you can shoot video without blowing out the footage is at dawn, dusk, or in other low-light conditions. It is highly recommended that you use a light meter to assess if the conditions are right for filming. A light meter will give you a precise measurement and will let you know if you need an ND filter, and if you do, which specific one to use. This will save you time and hassles later.

For photography, increasing the shutter speed usually presents no major issues you can't work around.

SYSTEM STATUS

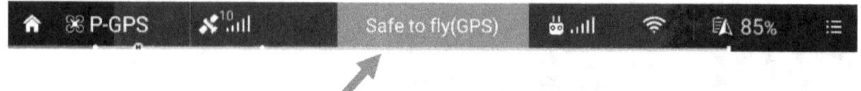

Tap on the System Status Bar to access the Aircraft or System Status screen, which is shown below.

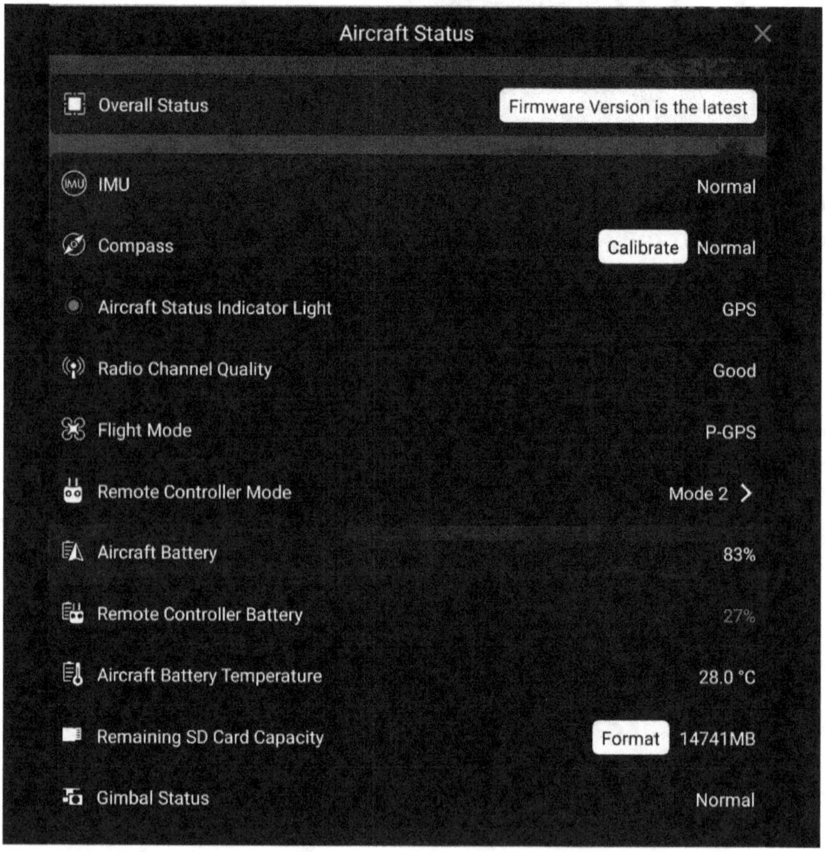

Aircraft Status	✕
▣ Overall Status	Firmware Version is the latest
⊛ IMU	Normal
⊘ Compass	Calibrate Normal
● Aircraft Status Indicator Light	GPS
⦿ Radio Channel Quality	Good
✖ Flight Mode	P-GPS
⚏ Remote Controller Mode	Mode 2 ❯
⚠ Aircraft Battery	83%
⚏ Remote Controller Battery	27%
🌡 Aircraft Battery Temperature	28.0 °C
▬ Remaining SD Card Capacity	Format 14741MB
🎥 Gimbal Status	Normal

The System Status screen provides a summary update on several key systems and settings, all of which are self-explanatory. If there is an issue or problem, you will see a warning or advisory message on the screen. You can also initiate Compass Calibration or Format the SD card by tapping the buttons.

TAKE-OFF

AUTO TAKE-OFF

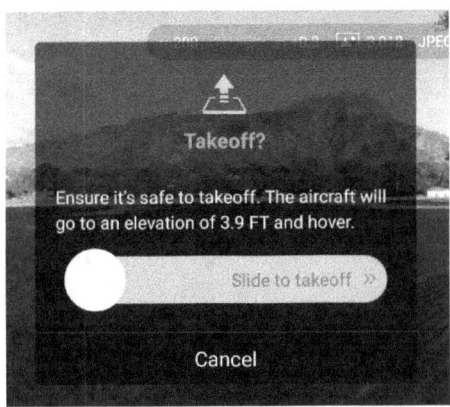

For Auto Take-Off, press the Auto Take-Off button, then slide the button at the prompt to initiate take-off.

MANUAL TAKE-OFF

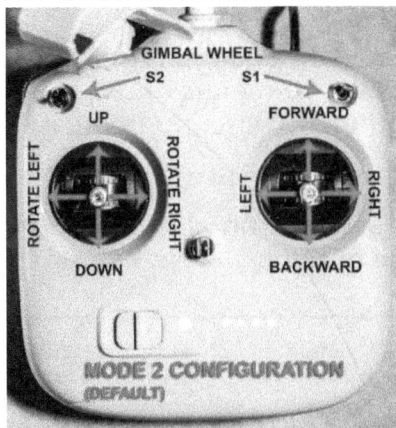

Push the Throttle (the left stick) until the aircraft starts ascending. Keep pushing the throttle until the aircraft reaches an acceptable height.

With either method, it is important to follow the Preflight Checklist before initiating take-off.

VIDEO SIGNAL (WI-FI)

This screen confirms your Wi-Fi SSID and allows you to change the password. By default, the password is 12341234.

The DJI Phantom 3 Standard operates within the range of 2.40 to 2.483 GHz.

In the United States, in accordance with Federal regulations, the Wi-Fi has a maximum range of 1,000 meters or .62 miles. The remote controller, while operating at a different frequency, has the same maximum range.

The maximum range of .62 miles assumes an altitude of 400 feet (or 100 meters) and a clear line of sight.

KEY SPECS

[refers to the Maximum values]

AIRCRAFT WEIGHT	2.7 pounds	1216 grams
ASCENT SPEED	11.2 mph	5 m/s
BATTERY RECHARGE	96 minutes**	
DESCENT SPEED	6.7 mph	3 m/s
FLIGHT DISTANCE	.62 miles	1,000 m
FLIGHT TIME	25 minutes	
SPEED	35.6 mph	16 m/s
WIND (unsafe to fly)	22.2 mph	10 m/s
SD CARD CAPACITY	16 Gb	
RAW (4:3) *	659 photos	
JPG (4:3) *	3,089 photos	
JPG + RAW (4:3) *	543 photos	
2.7K (30 fps) *	52 minutes	
1080p (30 fps) *	84 minutes	
720p (30 fps) *	210 minutes	

KEY
miles per hour = mph
meters per second = m/s
meters = m

* values for 16 Gb SD memory card
** approximate time with the standard 57-watt charger

99

CONVERSIONS

METERS PER SECOND TO MILES PER HOUR

METERS PER SECOND	MILES PER HOUR
1	2.2
2	4.5
3	6.7
4	8.9
5	11.2
6	13.4
7	15.7
8	17.9
9	20.1
10	22.3
11	24.6
12	26.8
13	29.1
14	31.3
15	33.6

METERS TO FEET

METERS	FEET
1	3.3
5	16.4
10	32.8
15	49.2
20	65.6
30	98.4
40	131.2
50	164.0
60	196.6
70	229.7
80	262.5
90	295.3
100	328.0
500	1,640
1,000	3,280

TIPS
(in no particular order)

START WITH A PRACTICE DRONE FIRST

Drones are expensive. Part of the fear of flying comes from knowing that if you make one mistake you could destroy the drone in a crash. And unlike a video game, if you crash it, it is a significant financial loss. Although the DJI GO app has a simulator, it is not the same as actually flying a quadcopter. Buying a small practice drone is one of the best investments and will increase your confidence and decrease your anxiety once you start flying more expensive machines.

START LOW AND SLOW

There is no reason to rush to unbox your drone and get it up in the air as soon as possible. Take your time, read this book and the DJI manual and take things slowly. Start with just turning the drone off and on, and when you are ready, start by hovering, then landing, and gradually fly higher and farther each time. Take your time and go slowly. There is no shame in flying twenty feet off the ground.

BE SURE TO REGISTER YOUR DRONE

The penalties for failing to register your drone are severe. If you should be involved in some kind of accident or other incident and the Federal Aviation Administration discovers your drone is not registered, you could be in trouble. Why chance it? Just register it.

GET A CARRYING CASE

Invest in a carrying case. There are a variety of options, including soft shell cases that do not require you to remove the propellers. A case will not only help protect your drone, but help prevent losing accessories.

FLY IN REMOTE, OPEN AREAS

When you fly your drone initially, choose the most remote locations you can find. This not only helps ensure the safety of others, but will help ensure the safety of the drone by giving it plenty of landing space. As your skill level increases, you can consider more challenging locations.

DO NOT FLY IN BAD WEATHER

Do not fly your drone in high winds, rain, or other adverse conditions. DJI defines unsafe winds as those more than 22 miles per hour, but when you are first learning, even winds at those speeds can be dangerous and disastrous, especially in A-Mode (ATTI).

DO FLY OVERS AND PRACTICE RUNS

If you are shooting video and are trying to get a particular shot, do fly overs and practice runs. This will help you get the best shots possible. When you do a fly over, look for areas that might be prone to aliasing too. You can either recompose the shot to avoid those areas or try moving in closer, which will either reduce or eliminate the aliasing.

FLY SLOWLY AND SMOOTHLY

For the best aerial video, it is important to fly slowly and smoothly. If need be, you can always speed the footage up in postproduction. Adjusting the Expo and Gimbal settings will help soften the controls and make it easier to get stable shots. Also, if it helps, the control sticks themselves can be raised and lowered to help achieve better stick control.

GET A GIMBAL LOCK / LENS COVER

The gimbal lock that comes with the Phantom 3 is difficult to put on and take off and does nothing to protect the lens. If you go on Amazon or eBay, you can find aftermarket gimbal locks that not only stabilize the gimbal during transport but also protect the lens. Just remember to remove it before starting the aircraft; otherwise, it can strain and overheat the gimbal's motors.

GET AN EXTENDED WARRANTY

Aerial drones are expensive and relatively easy to damage. Consider getting yourself an extended warranty. DJI offers extended care packages, but these tend to be expensive. You might want to look at getting a generic extended warranty such as those sold by Square Trade. It is usually a small price to pay for the extra peace of mind.

GET A LIGHT METER

It is highly recommended that you use a light meter to save time when installing ND filters. A light meter can confirm the type of ND filters you need for a proper exposure, and then you can conveniently install them early during preflight.

If you do not use a light meter, then you have to power on the aircraft, take a light reading using the GO app meter, shut the aircraft down to install the ND filters, and then power on the aircraft again. ND filters should not be installed when the camera is on as this can cause strain on the gimbal motors. In addition, the light meter on the GO app is limited in range as an exposure meter (± 2 stops max) and relies on the Phantom's camera, which is awkward to use in place of a handheld light meter.

GET ND FILTERS

For shooting video, if you do not get ND filters, you will only be able to shoot at dawn, dusk, and other low-light conditions, and then only for a short window of time. Because the camera has a fixed aperture of 2.8, you cannot stop down the aperture (that is, increase the F stop) to decrease the light coming into the camera, so the only practical way to decrease the light is by using ND filters. As of June, 2016, DitzCo of Chicago, Illinois sells an ND filter kit for $28.95. Enter the promo code 15OFFBOOK and you can receive a 15% discount. For more information about the kit, please visit: DITZCO.COM

NOTE: You do not need ND filters for photography, only video. For photography, you can effectively control exposure by using shutter speed. For video, adjusting shutter speed for a proper exposure is not a good option.

USE RECOMMENDED SETTINGS TO START

When you are shooting video, there are recommended settings you should seriously consider using. Over time and with experience, you may adjust them for your specific needs. For instance, if you want more of a film look, then you might decide to adjust the frame rate to 24 frames per second instead of 30 frames per second. These settings are only meant as a starting point.

[REQUIRE ADJUSTMENT IN POST]
ISO: 100
VIDEO SIZE: 2.7K
FRAME RATE: 30
SHUTTER SPEED: 60
WHITE BALANCE: USE A PRESET OR CUSTOM, NOT AUTO.
STYLE: CUSTOM (-2,-1,-2)
COLOR: D-LOG

The above settings will require further adjustment when editing. For instance, the 2.7K video will probably have to be down converted to a video size of 1920 x 1080, and shadows, mid-tones, and highlights will have to be adjusted to add contrast. Also saturation may also have to be increased. If you do not want to do any adjustments like that in editing, then you should follow the settings below as a starting point.

[DO NOT NECESSARILY REQUIRE ADJUSTMENT IN POST]
ISO: 100
VIDEO SIZE: 1080p
FRAME RATE: 30
SHUTTER SPEED: 60
WHITE BALANCE: USE A PRESET OR CUSTOM, NOT AUTO.
STYLE: CUSTOM (-2,0,0)
COLOR: USE ANY PRESET OTHER THAN D-LOG

You can still apply modest color corrections and grading to the above settings, but they should be subtle. It is suggested that you try to get the settings correct in-camera as much as possible to minimize the need for later corrections in post.

MAKE SURE THE PROPELLERS ARE TIGHT

If you frequently take the propellers off for safety or transport reasons, make sure they are tight before every flight. Do not assume they will self-tighten to the appropriate torque. Make sure to tighten them by hand. Also, the propellers are not the same and must go on the correct motor. Be sure to put the right propeller on the right motor. (Refer to DJI Manual page 7.)

SET THE CORRECT FAILSAFE ALTITUDE

This is a common cause of accidents, so as a part of your preflight check, make sure the Return-to-Home altitude is set to a safe height. Err on the side of making the altitude higher rather than lower. You never know when you might run into an emergency, so you want the altitude at a height that will avoid all possible obstacles.

TAKE ACTION ON A LOW BATTERY WARNING

As soon as you get a Low Battery Warning, take it seriously, finish shooting, and start heading home. You do not want to put yourself in a position where the battery reaches a critical level and immediately begins a straight descent. The whole purpose of the Low Battery Warning is to prevent a Critical Battery Warning from happening. The bottom line is this:

If you get a Low Battery Warning, wrap it up and come home.

GET SHADE PROTECTION

If you plan to shoot on a sunny day, you will need to get shade protection for your mobile device. Most mobile devices have screens that produce glare and make viewing difficult in daylight. Screen shades can be found online and elsewhere at a nominal cost. If you do not have one, you will probably have to position yourself so you are at least standing in the shade but still within line of sight of the aircraft. One of the most frustrating things in the world is to be flying over a great location but not being able to clearly see the screen.

KNOW YOUR BRAKING DISTANCE

Before you start flying in more adventurous locations, be thoroughly familiar with the flight characteristics of your aircraft. Be certain you know how long it takes the aircraft to stop in flight at different speeds. If you don't, then you might find yourself crashing into something you were trying to avoid. This is also why you want to be careful when making Expo and Gain Adjustments. For instance, changing the Sensitivity on the Brake setting from 100% to 80% can significantly increase the time and distance it takes to reach a stop.

DISABLE REMOTE

If you happen to have inquisitive people who might have access to your drone and might want to experiment with it when you are not around, or you just want to give the appearance of your drone being broken or disabled, then go into Master Stick Mode, select the Custom setting, but don't apply any functionality and leave everything unassigned.

If someone messes with your drone, everything will turn on, but the remote controller won't be able to activate anything, and the drone will appear broken or disabled. In addition, no warning or error messages will appear.

USE TWO MOVEMENTS AT ONCE

As your flying skill improves, start practicing patterns with both sticks at once. Some of the best and most professional shots are those that have the camera moving in two directions at the same time. For example, forward and up is more interesting than up by itself. Forward and down is more interesting than straight down.

FLY UPWIND

If you choose to fly the aircraft on a windy day, it is advisable to fly it upwind of your Home Point location. This way, if you run into a low-battery or other situation, you can fly the aircraft downwind to your position. If you fly downwind and get into trouble, then you will have to fly against the wind to get home, which will cause the aircraft to use more power.

USE CSC WITH CAUTION

Combination Stick Control (CSC) is when both sticks are pulled back to adjacent or opposite corners. The whole purpose of CSC is to create an unusual stick movement that requires a deliberate effort. In this way, CSC is thought to prevent a pilot from accidentally starting the motors or stopping the motors in flight. However, in our experience, if you use the CSC to land the aircraft, it might cause an abrupt increase in propeller speed and cause the aircraft to tip over. And, of course, you would never want to do a CSC in mid-air and risk stopping the motors.

In short, to land the aircraft, you may want to seriously consider using the left stick alone or Auto-Landing. In the DJI Manual on page 43, using the left stick or throttle by itself is referred to as *Method 2*.

We have found no issues with using CSC to start the motors.

AVOID ATTI MODE IN THE BEGINNING

One of the greatest things about the DJI Phantom 3 is that it can use GPS to hold a stable position in 3-D space. This means that while the aircraft is holding its position, you can make other adjustments in the GO app and not have to focus exclusively on flying. Think of P-Mode or P-GPS Mode as a form of Auto-Pilot.

A-Mode or ATTI Mode does not use GPS and while the aircraft will maintain its altitude, it will not maintain its position and will drift with the wind. Because of this, A-Mode or ATTI Mode requires greater skill and concentration.

As a student or new pilot, it is recommended that you use P-Mode in the beginning and only gradually experiment with A-Mode. And when you do experiment with flying in A-Mode, be sure not to do it on a windy day.

If you try to fly on a windy day, the aircraft will take off in whatever direction the wind is blowing and at the same speed as the wind, so it can quickly fly out of range and disappear.

ATTI MODE CAN CHECK WIND SPEED

Once you can fly safely in ATTI mode, you can use it to check wind speed. Just be sure you know how to fly in A-Mode (ATTI) and know how to regain control if you need to. By quickly looking at the horizontal speed indicator, you can gauge wind speed.

FLY BACKWARD TO AVOID PROPELLERS

If you are flying forward and/or into the wind, the aircraft will often pitch forward. When this happens, you will often see the propellers or arms of the aircraft in the top corners of your image. To avoid this, you can fly backward or away from the scene or subject, then reverse the footage in editing to give the appearance of flying forward.

DOLLY-IN SHOTS IN REVERSE

If you want to get a smooth shot of dollying into a subject or scene and do it safely, then you can have the actor get as close to the hovering camera as possible, then do a fly away in reverse, flying backward and up. When you reverse the footage in editing, the shot will show the camera gracefully descending toward your subject and end with a nicely composed close-up or medium shot.

USE RHYMES TO REMEMBER

There is much to remember when flying and filming with a drone, so this might seem silly, but it really helps to use rhymes to help you remember things. Here is one we created but feel free to make up your own. It relates to the status lights on the aircraft. Note: STF = Safe to Fly

Slowly flashing red.
The battery's going dead.
Slowly flashing green.
STF with GPS is what that means.
Slowly flashing yellow.
STF, but beware there's no GPS my fine fellow.

INDEX

iOS VERSION

The iOS and Android versions of the DJI GO app have a few differences but not enough to justify writing a separate book and manual for them. The layouts are slightly different. The iOS version has more descriptive text in one place and different naming conventions in another. Also, the iOS version has at least five features that the Android version does not. Here we will explore the main differences, but overall, they are virtually identical.

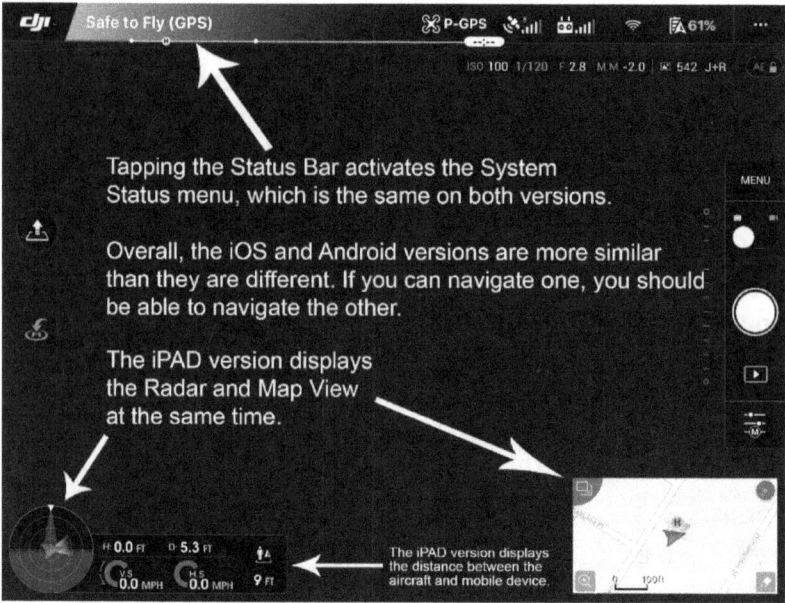

Visually, the iOS version has a sleeker and more streamlined appearance than the Android. The biggest difference is on the Camera View screen. The iPad shows both the Map View and Radar Screen at the same time. On the iPhone and Android versions, the Radar Screen is only shown when the Map View is hidden. Also, the iPad version displays an extra reading that shows the distance between the mobile device and aircraft.

FEATURE DIFFERENCES

Aside from the distance measure on the main screen, the iOS version has four other features the Android version does not, all of which can be found under General Settings.

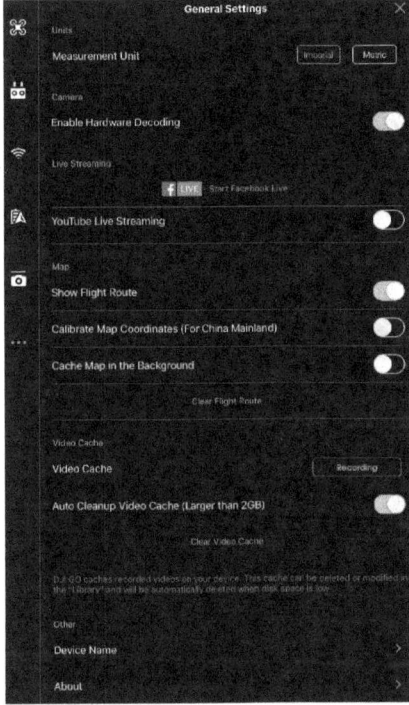

ENABLE HARDWARE DECODING
The mobile device processes the Wi-Fi signal instead of the software. This improves the video downlink signal and reduces lag time or latency.

LIVE STREAMING FACEBOOK
Connects to Facebook Live for video streaming.

YOU TUBE LIVE STREAMING
Enables live streaming to You Tube.

CACHE MAP IN THE BACKGROUND
Enables the map to be viewed when there is no cell service. This functionality is possible in the Android version, but there is no specific button to enable it.

DIFFERENT NAMING CONVENTIONS

For some reason, the iOS and Android versions use different naming conventions when describing the same basic gimbal functions and settings.

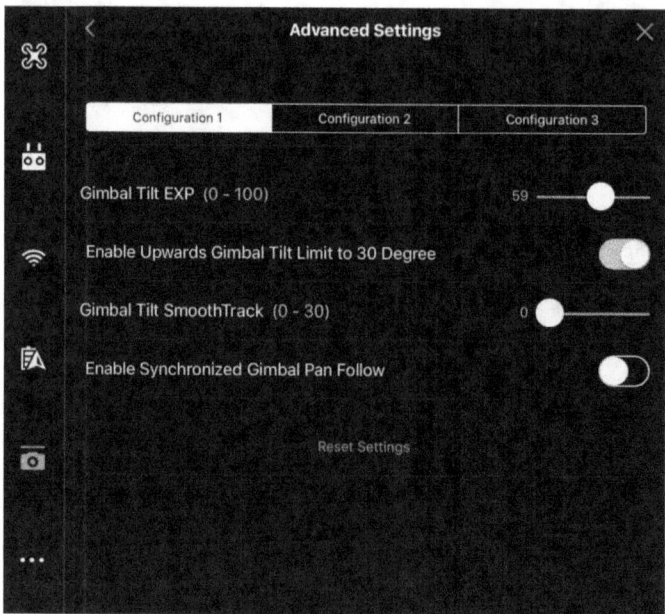

Refer to the chart below.

iOS	ANDROID
Gimbal Tilt Exp	Gimbal Pitch
Enable Upwards Gimbal Tilt	Gimbal Pitch Limit
Gimbal Tilt SmoothTrack	Gimbal Pitch Smooth
Enable Synchronized Gimbal Pan Follow	Gimbal Yaw Synchronous Follow

For most everything else in the iOS and Android versions, the naming conventions appear standardized across the other functions and settings.

DESCRIPTIVE TEXT

The iOS version has more descriptive text in the interface, especially on the Main Controller screen. This, of course, is helpful to explain what things do if you have forgotten or need a reminder.

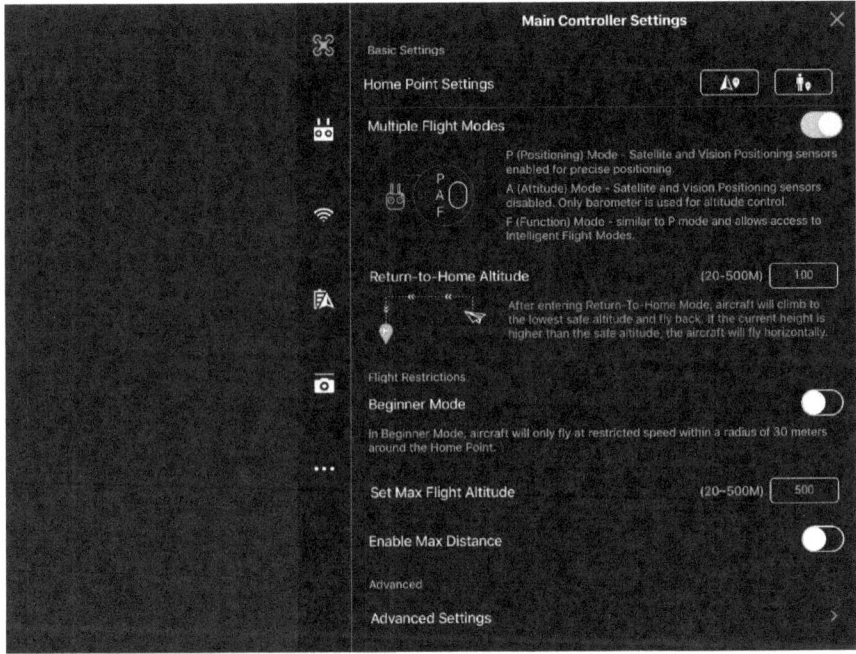

Overall, the iOS and Android versions are remarkably similar in terms of their functionality and location of controls.

If you can navigate one version, it should be relatively easy to find what you are looking for in the other.

Hopefully, as the apps continue evolving, the versions will eventually merge and have the same interface and location of controls.

NOTES

Visit us at
dji.server808.net